Chameleon Ware Art Pottery

A Collector's Guide to George Clews

Hilary Calvert

4880 Lower Valley Rd. Atglen, PA 19310 USA

Dedication

To Denis and Gnasher

Designed by Laurie A. Smucker
Type set in University Roman Bd BT/Korinna BT

ISBN: 0-7643-0577-8
Printed in China
1 2 3 4

Published by Schiffer Publishing Ltd.
4880 Lower Valley Road
Atglen, PA 19310
Phone: (610) 593-1777; Fax: (610) 593-2002
E-mail: Schifferbk@aol.com
Please write for a free catalog.
This book may be purchased from the publisher.
Please include $3.95 for shipping.

In Europe, Schiffer books are distributed by
Bushwood Books
6 Marksbury Avenue
Kew Gardens
Surrey TW9 4JF England
Phone: 44 (0)181 392-8585; Fax: 44 (0)181 392-9876
E-mail: Bushwd@aol.com

Please try your bookstore first.

We are interested in hearing from authors
with book ideas on related subjects.

Contents

Acknowledgments

My thanks are due to Len and the late Pam Brown, Colin Craig, Adrian and Amelia Holt, Atlanti Meyer and Laurence Poore, who have lent pieces from their collections to be included in this book. Thanks also to Ann Wallbanks and Dorothy and John Oliver for their help in my research, and to the many Clews paintresses who shared their memories with me.

Extracts from *The Pottery Gazette and Glass Trade Review* are reproduced by kind permission of Tableware International.

Introduction:
George Clews & Co. Ltd. 1906 - 1961

George Clews & Co. Ltd. was one of many potteries in Staffordshire, England, which produced brightly colored, hand-painted art ware at the beginning of the twentieth century. Yet Clews' Chameleon Ware is quite unlike other pottery of the time, and is immediately recognizable by its glowing colors, its exuberant designs, and above all by its silky semi-matt finish which makes it such a joy to touch. It is this glaze, produced after much experimentation, which distinguishes Chameleon Ware from its contemporaries, and enabled the company to run a successful art pottery alongside a commercial pottery business.

The name "Chameleon Ware" is said to have been chosen for the pottery "because it changed color in the firing." This may have been the reason for the name but, whether true or not, it certainly is a most attractive pottery. Chameleon Ware was produced in the main in a limited range of strong colors. However, the range of shapes was vast, and most were decorated with distinctive patterns which were hand-painted under the glaze.

This book traces the history of George Clews & Co. Ltd., the makers of Chameleon Ware. The pottery is one of so many which have disappeared during the last forty years. Until now it has been completely undocumented and, despite its relatively recent demise, no written records have been found. Much of the information included here has been compiled from primary sources during the past eight years. It relies on the memories of those who worked in the industry in their youth, and who have gladly shared those memories with me. They have often found it surprising that an interest is now being taken in Chameleon Ware, although also saying that it has been both undervalued and overshadowed by more famous names for too long.

As a collectors' book, *Chameleon Ware Art Pottery* includes a listing of all the pattern numbers which I have been able to identify, plus an example of each. In the absence of a pattern book, this is inevitably an incomplete list, and I would be delighted to receive any information which would add to it. I have also included many photographs of Clews' pottery which I hope will be of interest to existing Chameleon Ware collectors, and will perhaps encourage others to begin the search. The ware was widely exported from England before the Second World War, and no doubt much has crossed the Atlantic since then. Although not as easily found as some of the larger potteries' work, Chameleon Ware is still available at affordable prices from antique and collectors markets. The prices given in this book represent a range which might be seen in a dealer's window for an undamaged piece. Prices vary according to size and rarity of pattern, and are given as a guide only. The dimensions given are in inches, the height being followed by the width.

Chapter 1
The Potteries

The Potteries is the name given to the area enclosed by six towns in Staffordshire, England. These towns are Burslem, Hanley, Stoke-upon-Trent, Longton, Fenton, and Tunstall. This area has been the center of pottery manufacture in England since the earliest recorded times. There were plentiful supplies of coal, wood, and red marl clay to be found locally. Thus simple utilitarian earthenware could be made by an individual potter and his family, working at their cottage which would have a small kiln built in the yard to fire the pots. The late 1600s saw the first factory for the manufacture of pottery in Staffordshire. Two Dutch brothers, John and Philip Elers, made fine red teapots, cups, and saucers at Bradwell Hall near Tunstall. In the late eighteenth century came the beginning of the industrial revolution. Roads were improved and canals built so that white clay from the west of England and flint from the east coast could be transported to the Potteries. Improved transport throughout the country meant that the finished ware could be sold over a wider area.

During this time there was a great expansion in the Staffordshire Potteries. Better building materials and methods saw the end of a cottage industry and the beginning of small factories. Josiah Wedgwood began working in 1759 at Burslem and soon dominated the industry with his skill and experimentation. By the end of the nineteenth century, the giants such as Wedgwood had been joined by a large number of firms in the Potteries, each employing a relatively small work force. Workers moved quite freely and frequently between them, going from job to job as they sought a change of conditions or a better wage. At this time the industry was booming. Vast amounts of pottery were exported all over the British Empire and colonies. The Potteries was covered in a pall of black smoke from the coal-fired bottle ovens, and living and working conditions for the potters and their families were poor. Clay and flint dust in the lungs and lead poisoning from the glazes were health hazards throughout the industry, and it was not until 1913 that the first legislation was introduced to control working conditions for lead glazing. Dust extraction was not mandatory until considerably later.

During the first half of the twentieth century, the time in which George Clews & Co. Ltd. was in business, trade fluctuated. There were shortages and difficulties during the First World War, a period of expansion in the early 1920s, followed by the world depression of the late 1920s and early 1930s. The Second World War saw government legislation which meant the end of decorated pottery for the British market, and severe fuel shortages necessitating a cutback in kiln firing. In 1910, the six towns had united to form one city to be known as Stoke-on-Trent. In a similar way, the potteries have been combined since the 1960s into ever larger groups. Sadly, in the process, very many of the small potteries became commercially unviable and have either been swallowed up by the conglomerates or, as in the case of George Clews & Co. Ltd., have disappeared altogether.

Brownhills Pottery

George Clews & Co. Ltd. began as a pottery business in 1906. The Staffordshire Sentinel Directory for 1907 lists Clewes (sic), George & Co., at Progressive Works, Commercial Street, Burslem as a general earthenware manufacturer, making jet, samian and Rockingham teapots. Clews would seem to have stayed here only for a short time and by 1908 they had moved to Brownhills Pottery, Tunstall, where the company remained until it closed.

Brownhills Pottery was located alongside Brownhills Road, Tunstall, Staffordshire, just north of its junction with the present Canal Lane, in an area now covered by the car park of the tile manufacturer, H&R Johnson. The first occupier of the pottery, from about 1805, was Joseph Marsh, a china manufacturer. He was succeeded by Samuel Marsh (possibly his son) and Richard Heywood in 1817, trading as "Marsh and Heywood" until 1845. By 1846 the china manufactory was taken over by George Frederick Bowers, the quality of whose china goods gained a medal at the 1851 exhibition in London. Some time after 1851 Bowers began the manufacture of earthenware. He died in 1867 and was succeeded by his son, but the business did not prosper and was in liquidation by 1871. The pottery was then bought by James Earley of Alsager, and continued in his family as the Brownhills Pottery Company until 1896, when it was bought by Salt Bros., from whom George Clews & Co. Ltd. leased it in 1908.

The Inland Revenue Land Survey of 1912 describes the property as "part of manufactory," occupying fifty-six hundred square yards. The freehold owner was A. C. Salt, from whom George Clews had a seventy-seven year lease which had commenced in 1908. The rent paid was £100 per year and the gross value of the property was assessed as £1200. It was described as:

> Earthenware manufactory: 3 ovens, potters shops, warehouses, offices etc. Old and in very poor condition.

George Clews was born in Wolstanton, Staffordshire in 1842 and married Harriet Swinnerton. They had two children—a daughter Ada and on 24th July 1875, a son, Percy Swinnerton Clews. On Percy's birth certificate, his father's occupation is given as "Potter's Manager," and the family address as 40 Bedford Street, Shelton. On 10th March 1903, Percy Clews married Emma Hollin Bill at the Register Office, Stoke-on-Trent. The elder Clews' profession was then entered as "Potter's Mould Maker," while his son was a "writing clerk." As it is his name which was given to the company, it would seem possible that shortly after Percy's marriage, George Clews started his son in business. His occupation does not suggest that George was a wealthy man, but as the pottery buildings were old and in poor condition, Brownhills was perhaps an affordable small beginning from which an enthusiastic young man could make a good start. Apart from his name, George Clews is not subsequently mentioned in connection with the pottery although he

An aerial photograph, probably taken in 1959 or 1960, of Brownhills Pottery at Tunstall. The premises were not large, and by this late stage only one of the original four bottle ovens remained standing.

may, of course, have given help and advice at the beginning. He died in 1918, while living with his daughter Ada and her husband Frederick Weller in Ilford, Essex, leaving an estate of just under £1000 to be divided between his children.

Having leased the pottery for ten years, two business partners, Harry Barrington Preece and Percy Swinnerton Clews, bought Brownhills Pottery from the Salt family on 11th February 1918. The price was £1350, to be paid in equal shares. To do this, they mortgaged the property to the Leek and Moorlands Building Society, from whom they borrowed £1000 at 6 percent interest. The business must have prospered, because by 31st December 1920 they had paid off the money owed on the property and became joint owners of Brownhills Pottery.

The company of George Clews & Co. Ltd., was incorporated on 14th May 1906, and registered as "Jet Manufacturers." It was to be run by two partners. Percy Clews, who was the Managing Director—a businessman without a background in the pottery industry—and Harry Preece as the Sales Director. A third director was Daniel Capper, the Works Manager, a man with a life-long fascination with the chemistry of pottery glazing and firing. These three built up a successful pottery business, producing jet, Rockingham, and samian ware teapots. The clay used was the local red Staffordshire marl. There was a clay pit just behind the premises, but whether the clay was taken from it for use by Clews is not known. It was not a large pottery, but aimed to be self sufficient, producing all the teapot molds and seeing the making process through to the building of wooden crates into which the finished ware was packed in straw for transport to Tunstall or Longton railway stations.

Brownhills Pottery was built on a traditional "courtyard" layout. The original pottery frontage had offices on the left and a central arched cart entrance which was controlled by "Old Bill" from his lodge on the right. "Old Bill" always wore a bowler hat and gold-rimmed spectacles. He had only one arm and was regarded as a formidable character by those who knew him. The other three sides of the courtyard housed the making and decorating shops and the joinery where Bill Stretton was in charge of crate making. Three coal-fired bottle ovens were used to fire the pottery. The largest (no. 1 oven) was assessed as taking nineteen days to fill, or set in, and seven to empty, or draw. Firing took about two days, after which the oven had to be allowed to cool before the pottery could be removed.

By the middle of 1913, with the business well established in teapot manufacture, a separate line of art ware was started, to run alongside the commercial orders. This would have been instigated by Daniel Capper, whose interest was always to experiment with glazes. The aim was to produce on a commercial basis pieces similar to those only previously available individually from studio potters. The art ware was to be "offered to the trade at reasonable prices, so as to bring them within easy reach of all collectors and lovers of artistic pottery." *(Pottery Gazette,* 1st April 1915)

During the First World War, Daniel Capper left to serve with the North Staffordshire Regiment. He was wounded, but on his return to Clews the art pottery line, which had become known as Chameleon Ware, was gradually extended. During the early 1920s, the first pieces of hand-painted Chameleon Ware were introduced, decorated by a team of between ten and fifteen paintresses. The new art ware was made in a white earthenware body, unlike the red clay still used for teapot production. A large number of shapes were cast, dried, biscuit fired, hand decorated, dipped, and glost fired on site, to produce a wide range of mainly decorative items.

In July 1927, *The Pottery Gazette and Glass Trade Review* carried an illustration of three Chameleon Ware patterns (nos. 22, 58, and 61). It reports the winning of a gold medal and diploma at the Philadelphia Exhibition of 1926, for "originality of design," and writes of "orders drawn from practically every civilised country."

The Pottery Gazette

An illustration from *The Pottery Gazette and Glass Trade Review*, July 1927. By this date, ware was hand-painted under the glaze. Patterns shown here are: left to right, no. 53, no. 61, no. 22.

During the 1920s, Clews did not produce continuously throughout the year. The work force would be laid off after the Christmas orders were completed in December and the pottery would not re-open until the first week of March, when more orders were taken at the Pottery Fair in Blackpool. This led to a discontinuity of workers, who would find employment with other firms during the winter and not return to Clews when the pottery re-opened in the spring.

As was usual in the Potteries, George Clews & Co. retained a London agent. He was Mr. Frank Findlay, a man much respected in the industry, who had spent his early life at the Aller Vale Pottery in Devon. His showrooms were on the second floor of Gamage Building (a large department store) in Holborn, London, where Chameleon Ware, amongst other firms' products, was displayed to the trade. At the same time, agents were employed in Australia, New Zealand, and South Africa, and by 1914 the firm was exporting widely, thanks to Percy Clews' enthusiasm for foreign travel. *(Pottery Gazette, Aug. 1914)*

MR. FRANK FINDLAY

Mr. Frank Findlay. At his retirement in 1936 he was "one of the oldest and best known agents of the pottery trade in London" according to *The Pottery Gazette and Glass Trade Review*, October 1936. Mr. Findlay represented George Clews and Co. Ltd., amongst other firms, at his showrooms in Holborn, London. A good range of pottery was on display in several rooms.

Opposite page:
An illustration from *The Pottery Gazette*, April 1915. This is the earliest picture of Clews' pottery, and shows the glaze effects which were intended to reproduce studio pottery style. "Crystalline glass" refers to the glaze, not to the pots, which were earthenware. The colors can only be guessed at, but the shapes are familiar and were all still in production until the 1940s.

Sales of the ornamental ware increased in volume, until by August 1925 *The Pottery and Glass Record* reported that art ware had become the greater part of Clews' production, and the pottery was also expanding. Four additional patent kilns were built to cope with increasing demand.

In common with the rest of industry, the Potteries suffered in the general recession of the early 1930s. Clews was no exception, and a cryptic note in Daniel Capper's diary for April 1930 reads:

> General Meeting of Directors of George Clews & Co. Ltd.
> Present: P. S. Clews, H. B. Preece, D. Capper, J. Machin, D. Bates.
> Salaries: Preece and Clews £360. Capper and Machin £221.
> Loss on 1930, which was a very bad year, about one hundred pounds.

In 1936, the mineral rights beneath Brownhills were sold to Sneyd Collieries for £100. This allowed mining for coal beneath the pottery at a depth of not less than seven hundred yards, and must have provided a welcome income in the difficult times of the 1930s.

On 1st June 1933, George Clews & Co. Ltd. became a joint stock company, owned by Mrs. Jeanie Preece (wife of Harry Preece) and Percy Clews, who were each allocated two thousand £1 shares in the company.

In the early hours of 16th September 1934, a fire started in the packing house, near the main arched entrance to the works. Much damage was done to the glost warehouse, and large stocks of decorated vases were destroyed in the vase warehouse. However, firemen kept the fire from getting a general hold, using water from the outside water tower to douse the flames, and managing to prevent them from reaching the oil store.

Although damage to some parts was extensive, the office books and records were saved, and the production side was fortunately undamaged. *(Staffordshire Evening Sentinel, 17th Sept. 1934)*

Despite the fire—not an uncommon occurrence in the Potteries at that time—production was soon in full swing again, and continued until the outbreak of war in September 1939. Pottery manufacture for domestic use was closely controlled during the war and for some time afterwards. Between 1942 and 1952, pottery production was restricted to simple white, cream, or brown undecorated ware for the home market, in order to reduce labor costs and release workers for the war effort. Firms were, however, encouraged to produce decorated ware for export, as an inflow of foreign currency was of national importance. Potteries were "concentrated" together, nucleus firms absorbing others to reduce work forces and to conserve raw materials and fuel. Prices were controlled and output restricted. Clews was a nucleus firm and remained open, sharing its premises with Lingard, Webster & Co. of Swan Pottery, Tunstall. They continued to make domestic tea ware, particularly brown teapots, and also cube teapots, but the production of hand-decorated art ware came to an abrupt halt, never to restart. Wartime conditions in no way reduced the British need for teapots, cups and saucers, if only to replace those lost by enemy action. In January 1941, *The Pottery Gazette and Glass Trade Review* reported that George Clews & Co. Ltd. "were amongst many potteries who sent pottery to help the people of Coventry after the air raid."

Percy Clews died in 1942. He was succeeded by Hubert Alan Brown, a local solicitor's son. Alan Brown had been apprenticed to Wedgwood of Tunstall, and then joined Clews in 1933. He worked through every part of the pottery from the slip house, where he shoveled clay, to the sales office. He also attended the local technical college. Percy Clews had no children, and left the income from his shares in the business to his wife. The shares were to pass on her death to Alan Brown, whom he had obviously chosen as his successor in the pottery.

"One of the gutted warehouses in the building at the pottery and tile factory of Messrs. George Clews and Co. Ltd., Brownhills, Tunstall, where a disastrous fire broke out in the early hours of Sunday (16 October 1934) morning." *Photo courtesy of Staffordshire Sentinel Newspapers Ltd.*

Following the fire of 1934, which destroyed the whole of the factory frontage, a new two story building was constructed to replace the old three story one. Immediately after the war, in 1946, a five year reconstruction program was begun. A complete modernization of the pottery was to be undertaken, but done in such a way that production was not to be interrupted.

The first phase was to erect a two-bay Northern light building in the middle of the works. This housed a new "Birlec" electric glost kiln, the biscuit warehouse, and the aerographing shop. A second "Birlec" kiln was on the ground floor of the main front building with the glost warehouse and the decorating shop above. The making shops were re-equipped with the latest type of drying stoves and making machines. Once this was completed, more adjacent land was bought, and the factory extended so that there were five such bays, all under one roof with the making shop. An electrical substation was built and it was expected that the pottery would eventually be all electric. The building program was to be completed by 1952.

In 1948 the bottle ovens were still being used for biscuit firing to 1300° C and for some glost firing to 1100° C. Additional glost firing was done in a seventy foot long "Birlec" electric kiln. For this, the ware was placed on an eighteen inch nickel chrome steel belt for passage through the furnace. These belts were not very suitable for the high temperatures required for earthenware firing and proved costly as they had frequently to be replaced.

A photograph from *The Pottery Gazette and Glass Trade Review*, October 1948, showing the two-story factory front built in 1934 to replace the old building destroyed by fire. The top of a bottle oven can be seen behind the frontage.

By 1948, the coal-fired bottle ovens were still being used for biscuit firing at Clews, but glost firing (glazing) was done in a "Birlec" electric kiln. Here, "green" or unfired ware is loaded onto a moving belt which travels slowly through the kiln. In the foreground, plates are passing through an infra-red drying system. Photo: *The Pottery Gazette and Glass Trade Review*, October 1948.

Glazed teapots being unloaded as they emerge from the other end of the electric kiln. Photo: *The Pottery Gazette and Glass Trade Review*, October 1948.

Women putting handles on cups at Clews. On the benches are "boards" which were loaded with the required number of pots to form one or more dozen and then carried, often balanced on the head, to the next process. Photo: *The Pottery Gazette and Glass Trade Review*, October 1948.

A section of the teapot making shop. Photo: *The Pottery Gazette and Glass Trade Review*, October 1948.

The biscuit warehouse at Clews in 1948. Having been fired to a biscuit state, ware was stored here until it was required in the decorating shop. Photo: *The Pottery Gazette and Glass Trade Review,* October 1948.

Chameleon Ware in the 1920s and 1930s." Cube ware was still very important, and had been produced in an oatmeal glaze throughout the war. There was a range of jardinieres, bowls, and vases produced in a matt white glaze, or a "two tone" effect called "Regency." Vitrified hotel ware was another line on offer, and in 1948 the outlook was bright, with full order books and "at least two years' orders on hand." *(The Pottery Gazette and Glass Trade Review,* Oct. 1948*)* However, the rebuilding costs had been heavy and the company never really found its way post-war. At the end of 1956, the pottery was re-mortgaged to secure a loan of £15,000 and in 1959 a new private company—George Clews (Sales)—was floated with a capital of £1000 in £1 shares. This was an attempt to rescue the ailing company, and efforts were made to improve and modernize the products. A new design team of John B. Adams and his wife, Tina, was employed to try to revive a flagging range. Advertisements were placed in the trade journals in an attempt to promote sales. A new line called "Pirouette" was introduced at the Blackpool Fair in 1961. Good business was reported, but it was too late, and on 16 May 1961 a receiver was appointed and George Clews, general earthenware manufacturers of Brownhills, Tunstall, Stoke-on-Trent, went into liquidation.

The pottery remained empty for some years. The buildings were demolished in the late 1960s when the land was purchased by H & R Johnson Ltd. for £31,598. It now forms part of their car park.

Without the art pottery which had done so well before the war, Clews concentrated on domestic table ware which was decorated either by aerographing, lithographic transfers, or by a Murray Curvex semi-automatic machine which applied the decoration to the ware by means of a gelatin pad. The work force in the 1950s was estimated by Mr. Harold Johnson (office manager 1952-1960) to be between 125 and 150. He remembers "two old Majolica kilns, which were never used in my time, which would in all probability have been used to fire

With publicity like this, did they deserve to succeed? The company rarely advertised in the trade magazines, but in May 1960 this picture appeared in *Pottery and Glass.* The sales message is less than clear.

MAKERS OF EARTHENWARE DINNERWARE, TEAWARE, FANCIES, ETC.

look out for GEORGE CLEWS & CO. LTD.

Brownhills Pottery, Tunstall, Stoke-on-Trent-88431/2. Telegrams: Clews, Brownhills, Tunstall

Chapter 2

The People

Percy Swinnerton Clews

Managing Director

Percy was born on 24th June 1875, at 40 Bedford Street, Shelton, and named for his mother, formerly Harriet Swinnerton. When aged twenty-seven, he married Emma Hollin Bill, on 10th March 1903. He was then described as a "writing clerk." By 1904 he was Managing Director of George Clews & Co., a position he held until his death in 1942.

Percy Clews ran the business side of the pottery most successfully, building up and then consolidating a small firm which never over-reached itself, rarely advertised, and almost never appeared at trade fairs. On the other hand it "invoiced and corresponded in six languages, and exported teapots to all parts of the world." *(Pottery Gazette,* Aug. 1914) Percy was a fluent linguist and traveled widely. In an article published in the 1924 *Cox's Potteries Annual and Year Book,* he wrote of being served with tea brewed in a Staffordshire teapot, both in Patagonia and in a "small, very small, village in Poland, miles and miles from the railway line." He and his wife Emmie lived at "Parklands," Victoria Road, Tunstall. Percy was a pioneering motorist, a keen chess player, and had an interest in making wireless receiving sets to hear the early broadcast radio programs. He died at home, after several months of illness, on 2nd October 1942, aged 67. His funeral, held at Carmountside Crematorium, Stoke-on-Trent, was attended by representatives of all sections of the pottery industry. Percy Clews was "of a kindly and genial disposition, though of a retiring nature," according to his obituary in the *Staffordshire Evening Sentinel* in October 1942. As Honorary Secretary of the original "Teapot Manufacturers' Association" and Chairman of the "Jet and Rockingham Association,"

as well as a member of the "Pottery Research Association," he was well known and liked throughout his branch of the industry, but was always more concerned with keeping and filling an order book than with publicity, either for himself or his firm.

He is remembered by Mary Brennan, a paintress at Clews 1920-1930:

> Mr. Clews was a very little man, no taller than me. He used to ride to work on a ladies' bicycle. He used to have a laugh and a joke with us.

Sadie Maskery, a paintress 1925-27, said:

> Mr. Clews was a very short man. He drove a car but could hardly see over the steering wheel. He did not come to the factory much—kept himself apart.

The ladies' bicycle seems to have made an impression on the work force and was mentioned by several other people.

As Percy and Emmie had no children, at his death the interest on his shares in the firm passed to his wife. On her death in 1946, the five hundred shares went absolutely to Hubert Alan Brown, who was then Managing Director.

Harry Barrington Preece

Sales Manager

Harry Preece lived in Waterloo Road, Cobridge, Stoke-on-Trent. He and Percy Clews together bought Brownhills Pottery and began the business.

Daniel Capper
Works Manager

Daniel Capper, Works Manager at George Clews & Co. Ltd., and his wife, Gertrude.

"Always test, and always be making some experiment."

This bold injunction is found on the first page of one of the many notebooks kept by Daniel Capper, Works Manager from Clews' earliest days. It was an ideal he followed all his working life, first with George Clews and later at the Avon Art Pottery, where he was working when he died in 1946. He had a fascination with the chemistry of pottery glazes and it was his experiments which eventually produced the semi-matt glaze so characteristic of Clews' Chameleon Ware.

Laura Robinson
The Missus

Laura Robinson was born in 1890. She was the "Missus" in charge of the paintresses at Clews from the early 1920s until the mid 1930s and lived in Louise Street, Burslem. She was responsible for many of the designs on the pottery, and would do much of the outline tracing onto the pots before handing them on to other paintresses to complete. Her work was marked "L.R." on the base, and virtually any piece so marked will be expertly painted to a high standard. In 1932 she left Clews and went to work at Sadlers, a Staffordshire teapot manufacturers. She died in 1976.

Some confusion has been caused by the mark "L.R." It has been thought by some to be that of "Lottie Rhead" (Charlotte Rhead), who did produce designs on a freelance basis for many Staffordshire potteries in the 1920s and 1930s. This, sadly or otherwise, is not correct. There is no known evidence of any involvement of Charlotte Rhead in Clews' designs. Laura Robinson, on the other hand, had a habit of marking many of her own possessions and even the underside of her dining room table with her initials, always with periods after the "L" and the "R."

Others recorded as having prominent positions at Clews include:

1952—Mr. C. E. Lane, Sales Director, Mr. F. Garbutt, Art Director, Mr. H. Hulse, Works Manager, Mr. K. E. Goodwin, Company Secretary.

1954—Mr. Lane and Mr. Hulse were no longer with the company, Mr. Garbutt was Works Manager and Mr. H. Johnson was Office Manager.

Laura Robinson. "The Missus," who marked her work "L.R."

Chapter 3
The Ware Produced

The pottery made by George Clews & Co. Ltd. which is of interest to today's collectors of hand-painted pots is the brightly colored Chameleon Ware. However, the people of Tunstall who remember the pottery are far more aware of Clews as a teapot manufacturer, because teapots were the mainstay of the business for many years.

Teapots and Tableware

The iron-rich red marl clay found within the Staffordshire Potteries is ideal for the making of teapots. It is sufficiently plastic for good molding and withstands the quick temperature change which occurs when boiling water is poured into the pot. Staffordshire teapots have always had a good reputation for the excellent tea which they make.

Initially, in 1906, the majority of teapots were produced in a decorated pressed jet body. The red clay was dipped in a cobalt stained glaze which when fired became a fine jet black. For the first decade of the century, after the death of Queen Victoria, England was in mourning. Bright colors were no longer fashionable even for household items, and the black jet glaze was particularly popular. However, ten years later, samian and Rockingham ware had almost replaced jet. Samian teapots were the natural red color of the Staffordshire clay. The name "samian" came from the Roman red pottery of similar appearance. The teapots were coated with a clear glaze which allowed the natural red clay to show through. They were often decorated with a colored band of slip which made them brighter and less funereal than jet. Rockingham teapots were made from red clay, and had a slightly metallic brown glaze containing manganese. This was the standard Staffordshire teapot. The glaze is said to have been first developed at the Rockingham Works in Swinton, South Yorkshire.

Teapots such as these, made in red earthenware and coated with black jet or brown Rockingham glazes, were hand decorated, often with floral designs. Staffordshire red clay teapots have a reputation for making an excellent cup of tea, and their sale was the solid financial basis of the pre-war company. Photo: *The Pottery Gazette and Glass Trade Review*, December 1919.

A comprehensive range was offered. The *Pottery Gazette* quotes of Clews in April 1915:

> Teapots and teapot sets, coffee pots, jugs etc., which they supply in plain, decorated, mottled and other styles. They supply their teapots in all sizes from the half-gallon one with two spouts to the small individual one-cup size.

By December 1919 Clews was: "A firm that is well known in the teapot trade." At that time they were represented in London by Mr. F. J. Bennett, Gamage Buildings, London E.C. Styles on show there included:

> ...an all-green pot, and some interesting "cut up" patterns embodying red and gold. One of the best selling lines is a chocolate coloured pot, having a broad cream slip band from the shoulder upwards, upon which is applied a forget-me-not treatment. The samian ware is supplied with blue, green, salmon or white bands and with numerous supplementary decorations. In addition to teapots a special line in shaving mugs is offered, supplied either in white with a gold line, or white with a litho spray and gold line. *(The Pottery Gazette and Glass Trade Review,* Dec. 1919)

In July 1927, *The Pottery Gazette and Glass Trade Review* was describing a new range of decorated samian ware produced by Clews as:

> ...having wide bands of powdered colour, such as red, blue, green and orange, with over-applied leafage designs finished off by a hand-gilt tracery.

This was in addition to the "ordinary plain" Rockingham and samian which was still made.

Percy Clews wrote a short article for *Cox's Potteries Annual and Year Book* in 1924. He was the Hon. Secretary of the Jet and Rockingham Manufacturers' Association, and was describing the processes of the manufacture of teapots.

> The manufacture of these "common" teapots (common only, I hasten to say, in the sense that they are universal) is not at all a simple process, low though their costs to the user may be. The processes through which they pass are more numerous and more complicated than might be imagined. The body of the teapot, minus spout, handle and cover, is first made in two halves in moulds on the "jigger". This rough body then passes to the turner who, on his lathe, turns it to a smooth finish, and also turns in the verge on which the cover is destined to rest. It then goes on to the handler, who makes and attaches the handle and spout. In the meantime the cover has been rough made on a special "cover jigger", and also passes on to a turner, who rapidly turns it down to its exact shape and size. The coloured bands seen on "samian" teapots are blown on the pots in coloured slips by the turner whilst the article is in that stage of its manufacture.

"Colour banding on teapots at George Clews & Co. Ltd." A decoration of colored slip—clay mixed with water to a runny consistency—was blown onto the surface of some teapots. Photo: *Cox's Pottery Annual and Glass Trade Year Book,* 1926.

By 1926, George Clews & Co. Ltd. were advertising that twenty million teapots were made in the Staffordshire Potteries each year. Unfortunately, no claim was made for the number produced from their own factory.

In 1926, when this advertisement appeared in *Cox's Pottery Annual and Glass Trade Year Book*, the art pottery was selling well. However, it was the teapots, still the mainstay of the business, which were advertised. The "Elvers" referred to in the text should probably have been "Elers," the two Dutch brothers whose pottery at Bradwell Hall, begun about 1693, was not far from Brownhills Pottery.

The Cube Teapot

The cube teapot, which became popular in the 1930s, had in fact been patented as a design in 1917 by Robert Crawford Johnson, Managing Director of Robert Johnson & Co. (Leicester) Ltd. The pot was constructed so that the spout and handle did not project beyond the body. The spout was formed by a partition on the inside of the pot leading from a perforated hole near the base to a hole near the top of the pot. The handle was made by curving the opposite wall of the pot inwards, and making a vertical column which could then be held. The lid had a similar depression with a knob which was recessed so that the cubic outline was not compromised. The advantage of such a shape was to prevent damage to projecting spouts and handles and to facilitate stacking and storage. The design was recommended for hotels and restaurants and was taken up enthusiastically by shipping lines when it was found that the cubic shape, when extended to all tea ware, although not to cups, could be economically stored on board ship with minimal damage in bad weather.

George Clews & Co. Ltd. was one of several manufacturers who produced cube tea sets under license. In 1936 the Cunard White Star liner *Queen Mary* was equipped with glass and china. The firm of Stoniers of Liverpool were "suppliers of glass and china for ship and hotel use," as well as having a retail shop which sadly closed to the public in 1997. Clews supplied cube stoneware for morning tea and cabin use and it was backstamped "George Clews & Co. Ltd., Tunstall. Cunard White Star. Stoniers Liverpool." *The Pottery Gazette and Glass Trade Review* said, "It had a pale matt oatmeal finish and must be regarded as an achievement in the application of an artistic glaze to useful and inexpensive articles," which was always an aim of the firm. The sets comprised teapot, hot water jug, milk jug, and sugar basin, all in cubic form.

A cube tea set produced by Clews for Stoniers of Liverpool, for use on Cunard White Star Line ships. The set includes teapot, water jug, milk jug, and sugar basin. The cups, saucers, and plate are in the same semi-matte oatmeal glaze which was considered modern and artistic, but are of standard shape. Cubic cups seem to have been a little too advanced at this time, and there is no evidence that any matching cups or saucers were produced. Teapot: 3.5" cube. $160-$190. £100-£120 for the set.

A Clews cube teapot in oatmeal glaze. 3.5" cube. $105-$135. £65-£85.

In 1939 the RMS *Mauritania* was equipped with 8,500 pieces of oatmeal cubeware by Clews. Such large orders must have been of considerable benefit to a small company. Cubeware continued to be made at the Brownhills pottery throughout the war years, keeping the factory in production when only undecorated ware was permitted to be produced for the home market.

After the war, in 1946, the Cunard liner *Queen Elizabeth* sailed on her maiden trip, following a major refit after nearly six years as a troop transport. Over 150,000 pieces of British pottery and glass were aboard, the cubic stoneware again having been supplied by George Clews & Co. Ltd. The same oatmeal glaze, considered "artistic," was used, and the design, being both functional and attractive, was well received.

The Dripless Teapot

The IXL teapot, base marked with the patent no. 327254. A good teapot with a metal spout which pours very cleanly. Bought for £2 ($3.20) and now in regular household use.

A milk jug from a cube set in a shiny brown glaze. The base is marked "*Souvenir* CUNARD LINE. Made by George Clews & Co. Ltd., Tunstall, for Stonier & Co. Ltd., Liverpool." It would seem that passengers were expected to take small items home with them after completing a voyage. 3" x 2". $60-$65. £35-£40. The price of these cubic items made for Stoniers reflects the interest shown by collectors of ocean liner memorabilia.

Throughout the first half of the twentieth century, teapot manufacturers were striving to perfect a teapot which could be put down after pouring without leaving a drip of tea which would collect at the end of the spout and then fall onto the tablecloth. One such design was patented in 1929 by James and Thomas Clyde King. Their invention was a metal spout which was attached by means of a rubber washer to a hole in the front of a tea or coffee pot. They claimed that manufacturing costs would be reduced, because without a formed pottery spout the teapots could be placed closely together for firing in the kiln. The advantage to the user was that the sharp metal edge of the spout gave an instant cut-off after pouring and thus prevented any drip. The metal spout could be removed from the teapot for cleaning, and easily be replaced. Clews used this device, known as the IXL (I excel), under license from King, Sherratt and Lakin.

In 1950, an automated advertisement was touring china shops. It was referred to as "an ingenious machine for demonstrating a teapot which has a chromium plated attachment to the spout. In operation the hand (with the teapot in a horizontal position) moves slowly and deliberately up an inclined plane at an angle of about 45 degrees. Upon reaching the end of its run, the hand tilts the teapot forward, and the cup is quickly and cleanly filled. The pot is then brought to the horizontal position again, and the hand slowly descends to its former position. The public were clearly impressed by the non-drip spout, but also by the fact that the cup never overflowed nor the teapot emptied itself." *(Pottery Gazette and Glass Trade Review,* April 1950)

Post war shortages of supply continued to restrict production, but in 1952 *The Pottery Gazette and Glass Trade Review* reported "a limited number of IXL non-drip teapots (size 36's only) are now being produced again by George Clews & Co. Ltd., following the recent shortage of metal spouts."

A part tea-set which goes with the IXL teapot. The duck-egg blue color on the outside and peach color on the inside of the hollow ware was probably blown on with an aerographing machine. This worked in a similar way to an air brush. $15-$25. £10-£15 for the set.

The IXL (I excel) automated advertisement which toured china shops in the 1950s caused public interest in the never-emptying teapot and the never-overflowing cup. The point of the advertisement was the metal non-drip spout. Photo: *The Pottery Gazette and Glass Trade Review*, April 1960.

The Belisha Teapot

The "Belisha" teapot. This novelty teapot in the shape of a field gun was named after Mr. Leslie Hore-Belisha, Minister for War in the British government at the beginning of World War II. This example has an earthenware spout, although some have a metal "IXL" spout which represents the gun barrel. 6" x 9" x 4.5". $190-$240. £120-£150. The price reflects the fact that these teapots are sought after by novelty teapot collectors as well as Chameleon Ware collectors.

This field gun teapot is the only novelty shape produced by George Clews & Co. Ltd. The design was registered in 1940, which puts it at the beginning of the war, just as fancy goods were being restricted. The base of the teapot is stamped "BELISHA REG. No. 837446" and also has the "Clews circling the world" base mark. The name "Belisha" is that of Mr. Leslie Hore-Belisha who was Secretary of State for War in Great Britain from 1937 until January 1940. He had the considerable task of organizing the re-armament of a country ill prepared for a war which was imminent. He introduced conscription and modernized the army, and with his gift for public relations doubled the strength of the volunteer Territorial Army. However, his efforts made him unpopular with the older military establishment, and in 1940 he suddenly resigned. The reasons for his resignation were withheld from the public because the country was at war, and at the time there was considerable speculation in the press. None of this explains exactly why Clews made a teapot bearing his name, but his was the driving force which organized factory building for gun production and put the economy of Great Britain onto a war footing. The teapots were made in several pastel colors, including gray, fawn, blue, and green.

The DUB-L-DEKR

This ingenious design involved a teapot which stood on top of a hot water jug. The stacking had the advantage of reducing cupboard space required to store two pots when not in use but, more importantly, the heat rising from the hot water jug kept the tea in the teapot hot. It was produced in at least two sizes.

The aptly named DUB-L-DEKR stacking teapot and hot water jug. The date is unknown but would probably be late 1930s. The complementary shaping of the handles and spouts gives some style to an otherwise heavy design. 8.5" x 10" x 5". $70-$80. £45-£50.

The DUB-L-DEKR ready for use, with the teapot on the left and hot water jug on the right.

Tea for Two

A blue luster "tea for two" set. $130-$160. £80-£100 for a full set. With only one cup and saucer as in this case, $80-$95. £50-£60.

A teapot, milk jug, and sugar basin in cobalt blue. The teapot and sugar basin have silver plated, Birmingham-made lids with black knobs. $130-$160. £80-£100.

The small-scale tea services, known as "tea for two" and comprising a small teapot, milk jug, sugar basin, two cups and saucers, and a plate, were very popular in the 1920s and 1930s. They were used for early morning tea or breakfast in bed, and also for informal afternoon tea for two people. Unusually for a company which concentrated on production rather than advertising, Clews exhibited at the second year of the Empire Exhibition at Wembley in 1925. A special line of morning tea sets was produced and proved so popular that they had difficulty in keeping up with the orders. Sets were available in a pale or dark blue mottled glaze, in green with vermilion, and probably many other colors. There was also a blue luster, which was on a finer ware than the more usual relatively heavy earthenware body. On some sets, silver plated teapot and sugar basin lids gave an attractive contrast, particularly to the deep cobalt blue glaze.

An "ordinary" Clews teapot. Countless simple and practical pots such as this one with an oatmeal glaze and hand-painted flower sprigs must have been made and sold. Probably produced during the 1930s, it has little collectible value, but makes an excellent cup of tea. 6" x 9.5". $15. £10.

The hand painting on this teapot resembles that on the ornamental Chameleon Ware. Although it is unmarked and can only be attributed to Clews by style and design, it seems a "cross over" piece between ornamental and utilitarian ware. 6" x 9.5". $70-$90. £45-£55.

The "Perfecto" Teapot Set

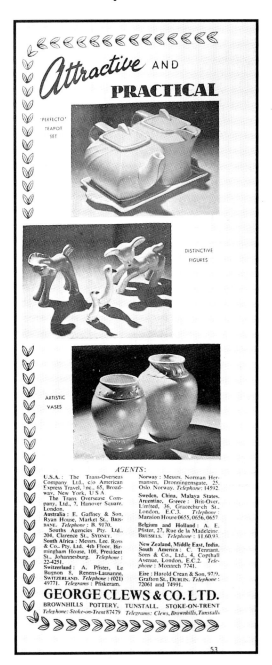

When this advertisement appeared in *The Pottery Gazette and Glass Trade Review* in January 1947, luxury items such as these were only available for export. The "Perfecto" teapot, jug, and tray set has streamlined decoration, presumably from pre-war days. Despite much searching, I have not found any examples of the little animals in England. They were probably all exported. Clews' foreign agents are listed at the bottom of the advertisement.

The "Perfecto" set had tea and water jugs side by side on a matching pottery tray. The design was streamlined and was usually decorated in a pale blue or green semi-matt mottled glaze. It was introduced before the war and then produced again in the post-war period, and was featured in one of Clews' rare advertisements in *The Pottery Gazette and Glass Trade Review* of January 1947.

The "Tudor Rose" tea ware, advertised in *The Pottery Gazette and Glass Trade Review* of April 1950. Although called a "new design," the heavy earthenware and floral design did not anticipate 1950s style.

DESIGNED FOR EXPORT

" Tudor Rose "
(Patent No. 1010. Pink)

One of many new designs being specially produced for the export market. It is a very attractive floral pattern based on traditional lines. The shape is " Stewart," and the ground is pure white. A delicate washband and gold lines give an attractive finish.

Made by Geo. Clews & Co., Ltd., Brownhills Pottery, Tunstall, Stoke-on-Trent.

Other teapot patterns were noted, but rarely illustrated. "Tudor Rose" had an "attractive floral pattern based on traditional lines, with a wash band and gold lines." "Windermere" was featured on the front cover of *Pottery & Glass* magazine in June 1950, showing a silk screen patterned tea set finished in pastel washbands, and available in several colors. The pattern was produced in tea, coffee, and dinner table ware, and was reported as exporting well in the dollar markets.

In the early 1960s, with financial problems looming, Clews made a final desperate effort to modernize its designs. A new range of "modern" tableware called "Pirouette" and designed by John Adams was introduced, and was advertised in the *Pottery Gazette*. Single colors were aerographed on the outside of ware, sometimes each piece being a different color to make a harlequin set. Clews showed these at the March 1961 trade show at Blackpool and along with the "exciting new ranges Portobello, Malacca, and Safari," they were said to be well received. However the firm closed before they had time to be marketed in any quantity.

The "Pirouette" range from *Pottery and Glass*, February 1961. A leap into modern design which could have brought success had there been time to market it before the firm went into liquidation in May 1961.

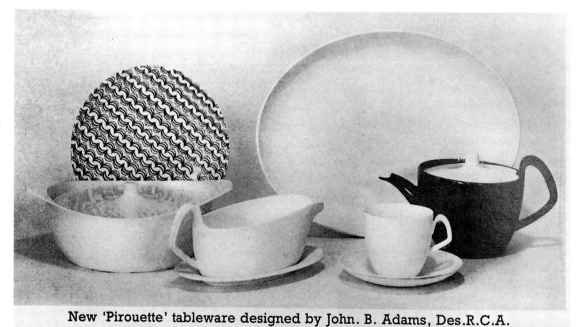

New 'Pirouette' tableware designed by John. B. Adams, Des.R.C.A.

Animals and Novelties

The *Pottery and Glass Record* of March 1931 describes "new animal figures of an unusual kind, mostly reptiles" being shown by Clews at the British Industries Fair. In October 1933 they are described as "rock garden ornaments." The reptiles are usually in mottled green, green with vermilion, or blue with vermilion. Those which have been seen include: a chameleon sitting on a log, a tortoise, a dragon, a baby dinosaur, a frog, a snake, a puff adder, a crocodile, and an elephant. It was presumably fashionable to have such reptiles appearing from behind rock plants and sunning themselves on the stones. It is unlikely that the glaze would stand the frosts of a British winter, so they would have to be taken inside as the night temperature fell.

In 1939 the *Pottery and Glass Record* refers to "developments in animal figures. Such are seen in the modern sculpturesque rendering of a Pekinese dog, sharp configuration, very impressionistic, and character-like poise. Better, perhaps, for characterization and elegance, is the delightful Golden Setter, available in a golden brown, or in white; distinctive, modern rendering. Bulldog is on similar lines. The Scottie model has a very good black, fine quality, glaze." In addition to the animals described, a brown and black streaked Alsatian dog has been seen, and also a small lion in all-over vermilion.

Chameleons do change color, but probably not to blue and orange. However, this version is highly collectible, and less common than the green one. 2.5" x 7.5". $175-$240. £110-£150.

A plain green mottled frog. Impressed mark "G. Clews & Co. Ltd., England." 2" x 4". $95-$130. £60-£80.

A green chameleon clinging to a log. This should be the flagship of every Chameleon Ware collection! Not the most beautiful of representations, but nicely bug-eyed. 2.5" x 7.5". The most expensive of the animals, because it is a Chameleon. $160-$210. £100-£130.

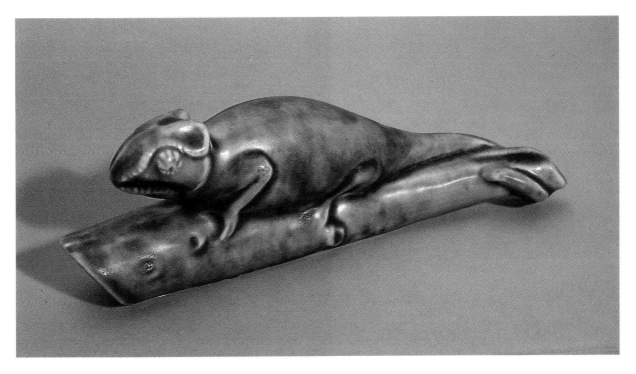

25

A slightly more life-like frog with stronger brown mottle marks. 2" x 4". $95-$130. £60-£80.

An oddity. It could be a sort of turtle, or it could be a baby dinosaur, or maybe just an imaginary beast. 4" x 7". $110-$135. £70-£85.

An animal usually identified as a dragon because of the folded wings along its back. One of the more attractive reptile shapes. 2.5" x 8". $120-$145. £75-£90.

A green crocodile, rather small and kindly looking. 1.5" x 6". $110-$145. £70-£90.

The dragon with fiery orange colored wings. Unmarked, but very obviously Clews. 2.5" x 8". $120-$145. £75-£90.

A puff adder in sinuous coils. Marked "PUFF. ADDER. G. CLEWS & CO. ENGLAND" on the base, in case there was any doubt. 2" x 5". $110-$145. £70-£90.

A tortoise, colored green and orange. A happy addition to any rock garden. 2.5" x 7". $110-$145. £70-£90.

A green working elephant, African by the length of his ears, with a wicker basket of fruit strapped to his back. Unmarked, but undoubtedly Chameleon Ware by the mottled glaze. 3" x 4". $145-$175. £90-£110.

Patterns seen are:

100 - yellow (often brown-flecked like an overripe banana)
101 - green
102 - brown
103 - pale blue
105 - dark blue
106 - slate green

A "leather" bottle, marked "Reproduction of Persian Art." 5.5" x 5". $150-$190. £95-£120.

Archeological excavations and the finding of Tutankhamen's tomb led to the popularity of Egyptian and Middle Eastern designs during the 1920s. In response to this, Clews produced a series of jugs in the style and texture of ancient leather water bottles. They have an embossed scroll pattern on each side, which might resemble tooled leather, and an abstract Art Deco panel painted under the lip. Embossed on the base is "Reproduction of Persian Art." The jugs have pattern numbers 100 upwards, according to color. This is a departure from the usual Clews' numbering system where the initial number refers to the pattern.

As a Christmas novelty in 1926, Norris, the Hanley wine merchants, bought a number of these jugs from George Clews & Co. Ltd., and sold them full of wine or port with an added cork stopper. Two, given as wedding presents to a bride and groom on 9th December 1926, are still proudly kept in a house in Stoke-on-Trent.

Another style of "Persian" jug produced is an upright shape with an overall pattern embossed in the casting mold. The sides are painted with a floral design and the handle has a fox's head where it meets the rim of the jug. The base is embossed "Reproduction Old Persian," and patterns 157 and 227 have been seen.

A more extreme novelty jug is the reproduction of a Graeco-Celtic flagon of 450 BC, with creatures on the handle, lid, and spout. The original on which it was modeled was a bronze flagon found in Lorraine, France in 1927. This was part of the "Basse-Yutz Find," named after the village in which the discovery was made, near the Moselle river. Some workmen constructing a road dug up two flagons and two urns, and all four pieces eventually found their way into the British Museum collection and are now on view in London. The metal flagon was a masterpiece of Celtic art, standing 14" high and inlaid with red glass and coral. The body was made from beaten bronze, but the spout, lid, and handle were cast, which allowed complex patterns to be formed. *The Pottery and Glass Record* of March 1931 reported that Clews had produced "a flagon which has a dog formed in the handle. The dog is watching a cat on top of the lid. The cat, in turn, is watching a bird perched on the spout!" When looking at the Clews pottery copy, this would seem to be the case, but cast pottery cannot have the detail of cast bronze. The original is thought to have a dog on the handle, but has two similar animals, possibly the dog's puppies, on the lid. The bird (which is obviously a duck on the original bronze flagon) is not being stalked by them, but is swimming happily up the river of wine which would have issued from the spout. Within the possibilities of plaster molds and cast pottery, Clews produced a very creditable two-thirds scale copy of the original. The lid was simplified so that it had one animal instead of two, but complex patterns on the bronze flagon were at least represented on the pottery surface, although lacking the sharp detail of the original. Clews flagons have been seen in plain color mottled glaze, or in numbered patterns, particularly number 11 (flame).

Detail of the dog, cat, and bird on the lid of the Graeco-Celtic jug below.

A lidded jug first made by Clews in 1931. It is a copy of a Graeco-Celtic flagon which was excavated in Lorraine, France. The dog on the handle is chasing a cat (or other animal) on the lid, which is watching a bird on the spout. The dog has a pierced muzzle. On the original jug a chain went through the hole and the other end was joined to the lid so that it would remain attached to the handle when not in place. The handle is disproportionately flimsy for the weight of a jug full of liquid. The shape of the body of the jug is very elegant, and it pours excellently. The base has the embossed words "Graeco-Celtic Flagon 450 BC" round the rim This example has a thick and treacly green glaze, splashed with vermilion which runs down the side and mixes with the green. 11" x 7". The handle on this jug has been broken in several places and it was bought for $70, £45. Intact, I would expect to pay $300+, £180+, especially if it had a painted design. They are rarely found.

During 1931 an Exhibition of Persian art was held at Burlington House, in London. The British Pottery Manufacturers' Association and the Stoke-on-Trent Rotary Club organized an excursion to London from the Potteries, so that those involved in pottery decoration could view the Persian art treasures at the Royal Academy. Nearly six hundred people made the trip and the patterns seen must have made a considerable impression. In the smaller potteries where trained designers were not employed and patterns were produced from the imagination and experience of senior paintresses, the Persian influence was much in evidence after the visit.

Embossed Designs

A small number of embossed designs, produced in the mold when the ware was cast, were made during the 1930s. An Art Deco horse prancing in a wavy sea with a "sunburst" sunrise beside it is one such design. On vases of smaller diameter, the sunrise appears without the horse. On most pieces, mottled green, blue, or oatmeal glazes were used, and a pink has been seen as well. On one exceptional vase the whole scene has been painted in bright colors. Whether this is a "one off" or a color variation, is not known. It is certainly most attractive. The sea and sunrise design with a sailing ship appears on a diamond shaped ashtray, again seen in mottled green and sometimes with the sun touched with vermilion. It was also produced on a vase which has been seen in mottled green and in oatmeal glaze.

Other raised designs include a water-lily which fills almost the whole of a plate. This has also been seen on a set of small dishes which fit on a wooden tray. There is also a complex design of fish and seaweed which graces a fifteen-piece fish set. This has been seen in oatmeal, pale blue, and gray.

The horse in the sea on two sloping-sided vases. The plain pink glaze on the left is an unusual color for Clews' pottery. 7.5" x 5". $90-$120. £55-£75 each.

A most unusual variation on the sea horse vase. The scene has been painted in underglaze colors giving a bright and lively result. 9" x 7". $320+. £200+.

The most "Art Deco" design produced by Clews. The embossed horse is galloping through the waves at dawn. On either side of the horse, the sunburst pattern is just visible. 9" x 7". $160-$240. £100-£150.

29

Detail of the horse on the colored sea horse vase (previous page).

An embossed "Art Deco" pattern in a mottled green glaze. This side shows the sailing ship. The sunrise is on the reverse of the pot. 9" x 7". $95-$160. £60-£100.

An embossed "Art Deco" pattern in oatmeal glaze, of a sailing ship on a wavy sea at dawn. 9" x 7". $95-$160. £60-£100.

An ashtray, with the ship and sunrise pattern in mottled green. 3.5" x 8". $55-$90. £35-£55.

Tableware

Clews must have made a vast quantity of ordinary tableware, which was bought for everyday use. Such items have not survived as well as the decorative pieces which would have cost more to buy, and would therefore have been more valued and cherished.

An elegant scrolled embossed pattern on a large pot which would grace a fireplace. 10" x 10". $130-$160. £80-£100.

A salt, pepper, and mustard set on a small tray. Neat, tidy and useful, in a fashionable mottled green glaze. No doubt many were sold at a moderate price in the 1930s. 2.5" x 4". $70-$90. £45-£55.

A plate with a simple but attractive embossed water lily. The style could be 1960s, but the circular "Chameleon Ware" backstamp suggests that it is pre-war. 7.5". $25-$40. £15-£25.

Left: A sugar and cream set, ready for a strawberry tea. The hole size of the sugar sifter requires caution in use, or else a very sweet tooth! Oatmeal glaze with tiny on-glaze painted flower sprig and blue dot. Much in the style of Susie Cooper. 5" x 9.5". $65-$90. £40-£55. Right: A toast rack with Deco detailing and a depression at either end for butter and marmalade. Oatmeal glaze, very practical for breakfast in bed, although the toast holding area is minimal. 4" x 8". $55-$65. £35-£40.

Four egg cups on a stand with a metal carrying handle and early plastic knob. 5" x 8". $40-$55. £25-£35.

A small posy bowl for a tray or table decoration. Mottled pale green, "George Clews" marking. 1.5" x 6". $15-$25. £10-£15.

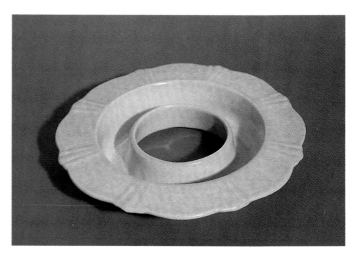

A ring posy bowl. The previous one will sit in the empty centre, but may not have been intended to do so. The two pieces were found in separate towns in England, and are probably unconnected. 1.5" x 9". $25-$30. £15-£20.

A small vase of impeccable design. In mottled pale green and marked "George Clews & Co. Ltd." but not "Chameleon Ware," it probably dates from the early 1960s. 4" x 3.5". $15-$25. £10-£15.

A fish set, consisting of six dinner plates, six side plates, a serving plate, and a sauce boat and stand. In oatmeal glaze with a fish and seaweed pattern embossed on all the pieces. $160-$240. £100-£150 for the set.

Nursery Ware

In common with other manufacturers, Clews found that bright transfer prints of nursery rhyme subjects had a ready market in the 1950s and could be easily and quite cheaply produced. This printed ware in no way matched up to the pre-war hand decorated designs, but no doubt served well to keep the work force employed, and its use gave pleasure to many children.

A flower holder intended for the bottom of a vase or deep bowl. Dark blue glaze streaked with brown. 3" x 4". $30-$40. £20-£25.

"Mary, Mary, Quite Contrary." Simple transfer-printed nursery ware such as this bowl was produced by Clews post-war. The transfers were bought from a transfer making company, and the identical pictures can be found on ware made by other potteries. 1.5" x 7.5". $15-$25. £10-£15.

Left: A white flower vase of questionable design and inferior earthenware. It was produced towards the end of the company's life, and would have sold very cheaply. 7" x 10.5". $8. £5. Right: A small white vase of good quality—simple but beautifully shaped. 3.5" x 3.5". $15-$30. £10-£20.

"Hazel Nutt With Her Pram." Transfer-printed nursery ware, produced under license from "G. B. Animation." Presumably part of a Nutt family set, as the back is marked "Ginger Nutt." 7". $15-$20. £10-£12.

Chapter 4

Artistic Ware

The Art Pottery

After George Clews & Co. Ltd. had been established as makers of domestic teapots for almost ten years, the decision was taken just before the First World War to diversify into the production of art pottery. They were not alone in this; many other potteries were doing the same. At Clews, however, it would probably have been the idea of Daniel Capper, the Works Manager, who was keenly interested in experimenting with the chemistry of pottery glazes and firing.

The Pottery Gazette of August 1914 refers to: "A special line of art ware on which they have been working for the past twelve months, and which bids fair to make a name for itself in the very near future..... less than a year ago they proceeded to give their attention to the manufacture of a class of art pottery which should be a cornmercialisation of crystalline and opalescent glazes, rouge flambés etc." The aim was to manufacture commercially glazes similar to those which had previously been produced only on individual pieces by studio potters. Industrial production would enable the company to bring prices "well within the reach of the middle classes."

An early shape with a turquoise glaze splashed and veined in gray. Hand inscribed base. 11" x 5". $130-$160. £80-£100.

An early Chameleon Ware pot with a green veined crystalline glaze. "Chameleon ENGLAND" inscribed by hand on the base. Mold no. 224. 8.5" x 5". $130-$160. £80-£100.

A streaked blue on brown vase. Unmarked base, but a very recognizable Clews shape. 6.5" x 4". $65-$95. £40-£60.

Probably the same glaze as the pot shown at bottom left, but a different and more subdued result. The word "ENGLAND" has been impressed into the base, as well as the usual "Chameleon Ware." Mold no. 219. 8.5" x 7.5". $65-$95. £40-£60.

Blue, brown, green, and yellow have run together in a controlled splash effect glaze. "Chameleon Ware," with the "C" elongated to underline "Chameleon," impressed by a stamp on the base. The shape, mold no. 219, was obviously popular and was continued for many years. 8.5" x 7.5". $95-$130. £60-£80.

Three Chameleon Ware pots showing different crystalline glaze colors— green, gray, and blue—all with impressed base stamps. Left; 8.5" x 5". $130-$160. £80-£100. Centre: 3.5" x 4". $50-$65. £30-£40. Right: 3.5" x 7.5". $65-$95. £40-£60.

A small green "art glazed" pot. 3.5" x 4". $50-$65. £30-£40.

An egg-shell glaze, possibly the one referred to by *The Pottery Gazette* as "similar to a robin's egg." 3.5" x 4". $40-$50. £25-£30.

37

A large pot with a blue and green glaze. The visual effect is of old beaten bronze. Impressed base mark. 9" x 8.5". $160-$175. £100-£110.

Two rare bronze luster vases, probably the "semi-matt bronze rouge flambé" noted in *The Pottery Gazette* in 1914. The luster was formed as metallic salts were deposited on the surface of the glaze when the pottery was fired in a reducing atmosphere, i.e. one lacking in oxygen. To achieve this, the air inlets of the glost oven were blocked once a high temperature was reached, so that the oxygen inside was depleted. The taller vase has a very early hand written impressed base mark. The two-handled vase has the slightly later stamped impressed "Chameleon Ware" mark. Left: 11" x 5". $160-$175. £100-£110. Right: 8.5" x 7.5". $160-$175. £100-£110.

Pink luster laid over the flame pattern. The interior of the pot is sandy brown, which would mean that the pattern is light and dark brown under the luster. The impressed base mark indicates that this is a very early occurrence of a painted pattern. The painted mark is 11/127. The flame pattern is as expected for number 11, but the exact color represented by 127 is unclear. 3.5" x 4". $80-$95. £50-£60.

A bowl in an unusual speckled glaze which is predominantly vermilion on the outside and yellow on the inside. Safety regulations would not permit this uranium glaze to be used today. The base mark is "CHAMELEON ENGLAND," impressed in typeface. 2.5" x 6". $65-$80. £40-£50.

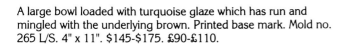

A large bowl loaded with turquoise glaze which has run and mingled with the underlying brown. Printed base mark. Mold no. 265 L/S. 4" x 11". $145-$175. £90-£110.

Two "splashed" vases both with printed base marks. Left: Blue with orange and yellow. Mold no. 210 M. 9" x 4". $90-$105. £55-£65. Right: Green with orange and yellow. Mold no. 202. 5.5" x 4". $65-$70. £40-£45.

A small, yellow glazed pot splashed with vermilion. 4" x 3". $40-$50. £25-£30.

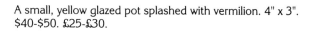

A heavily glazed vase of many colors. Blue with red and some yellow have been run together in a thick glaze, which has spread unevenly to give a treacly texture. Not a typical piece of Clews, but attractive as a piece of art pottery. 7" x 7". $105-$135. £65-£85.

The new art ware was produced on a white body instead of the red clay used for teapot manufacture. The glazes were described by *The Pottery Gazette* as "lustred and splashed and veined," and "a semi-matt bronze rouge flambé." Clews were said to be "the first firm who have struck a matt surface to the rouge flambé." "A line remindful of Hispano-Moresque, having a raised enamel line decoration." "A vellumed glaze with a rouge flambé painting." "Egg-shell glazes (one with the number L.1262), with a speckled appearance similar to a robin's egg." *(The Pottery Gazette,* Aug. 1914)

Buyers were assured, however, that the firm had no intention of reducing the effort going into the production of teapots, which would continue to be the staple line of business. At first only small pieces were made with the new glazes, but by mid-1914, after a period of trial, they were sufficiently confident to produce ware up to eighteen inches in height. These early glazed pieces have "Chameleon England" impressed into the base, either in typeface or hand printed letters, or "Chameleon Ware" impressed in flowing hand written characters, with the "C" extended to underline the word.

By April 1915, the range was more extensive. "Modern art vases, flowerpots and bulb bowls in various metallic, opaline, crystalline and aventurine glazes, and also a raised line decoration, finished in Rouge Flambé." *(The Pottery Gazette,* April 1915*)* The designs were carefully adapted to suit the shapes of the pieces, and were sold at "a few pence" for small items, grading upwards to "a moderate number of shillings" for the larger pieces. Each pot was unique, as exact reproduction was impossible, and mention was again made of the fact that prices were to be kept within easy reach of all collectors and lovers of artistic pottery.

Chameleon Ware

The name Chameleon Ware had been given to the glazed art pottery from the beginning in 1914. By the early 1920s, Daniel Capper had returned from the war and was ready to start a new line, which was to be hand-painted art pottery. Most of the pieces were decorative rather than functional, and included vases of all shapes and sizes, jugs, bowls, decorative plates, and wall plaques.

The Making Process

Casting Hollow Ware

The ware was slip cast in plaster of Paris molds in the molding shop which was "down the yard." Liquid clay or "slip" was poured into hollow molds. As the slip dried, water was absorbed by the plaster so that a solid crust formed around the inside of the mold. The excess slip was then poured out, leaving the shape of the article. The molds gave an impressed base number running from 200 to 400, sometimes with an S, M, or L denoting small, medium, or large versions of the same shape.

Drying

When the cast had dried sufficiently to shrink a little, the mold was taken apart, releasing the article. It was then "fettled" to smooth the seam marks, before being put in a warm drying machine. Once dry, it was ready for biscuit firing.

Forming Flat Ware

Plates were formed from flat slices of clay called "bats." A bat was pressed down onto a revolving "jigger" machine which shaped the inside of the plate. A profile tool then was pulled down to form the shape of the back of the plate as it revolved. The edges were trimmed and the plate was removed from the jigger ready for drying. At this stage, the pieces were known as "green ware" and were quite soft.

Laura Robinson or another experienced paintress would take a piece of biscuit ware and mark the pattern onto it in black pencil, which would fire off in the kiln. The placing and height of each section of the pattern was marked, as well as the positioning of the border. The patterns were usually based on stylized flowers or leaves, each with a border which complemented the main pattern. The outline was then painted on in black or brown with a fine lining brush, and the pattern and color numbers painted on the base. The pot had to have been biscuit fired to just the right hardness. If over-fired, it would feel smooth to the touch and the colors would run when applied. Correctly fired ware had a slightly rough surface which would absorb color when painted.

Biscuit Firing

Placing saggars inside a bottle oven. Saggars filled with ware to be fired were carried balanced on the placer's head. Each man had a roll of old silk stocking pushed inside his cap to help protect his head, as a full saggar could weigh fifty-six pounds. They were piled from floor to ceiling in stacks called "bungs." Placing was a very skilled job because different parts of the bottle oven reached different temperatures, so the ware had to be in the correct area of the oven for its type and size. As the oven floor was not level, the piles of saggars had to be carefully balanced. Photo: *The Pottery Gazette and Glass Trade Review,* March 1939..

Firing pottery in a coal-fired bottle oven was a skilled and complex process. The ware was put in fireclay boxes called saggars, to protect it from the direct flames of the oven. Saggars were carried into the oven and carefully piled from floor to ceiling in stacks or "bungs."

A full saggar would weigh about fifty-six pounds, and an oven could contain two thousand saggars. When the bottle oven was full—and filling took twelve, fourteen, or seventeen days at Clews depending on which of the bottle ovens was being used—the doorway was bricked in and the fire lit. The fireman was considered a most important person at the pottery. On his skill in adjusting the temperature of the fire depended the success of two or three weeks' production. He would stay on site during the two days of firing, keeping a careful watch on the fire-mouth, ready to add fuel or open and close

dampers as required. At the beginning of the firing, the temperature was kept low while the moisture in the ware was driven off. It was then allowed to rise until, after about forty-eight hours, it peaked at between 1000 and 1250 degrees Centigrade. After being held at that temperature for two or three hours, the fire was allowed to go out. Experience in firing was all-important. Trial pieces could be checked by removing a brick from the side of the oven and taking out a specially placed test piece. "Seger Cones," which changed in color from dull red through a standard color range to bluish white as the temperature rose inside the oven, were used as an indication, but temperature control was inexact, particularly as it varied in different parts of the oven. When the firing was over, the door was broken down and the oven left to cool. The biscuit ware was then removed and stored in the warehouse until required for decoration.

Decorating

A team of between ten and fifteen paintresses was employed to decorate Chameleon Ware. They sat in the same room as the teapot decorators, but at different tables. The two groups did not mix their work. Patterns were originated by Daniel Capper or by Laura Robinson, the "Missus," who recorded them in her book. The design filled the whole of each piece, covering all the available surface. Patterns were adapted to suit varying shapes of ware, so that the same design would give a totally different result on a convex piece from a concave one. Some parts of the pattern could expand out of recognition round the border of a plate, or contract into almost nothing in the center of it.

Ware was carried around the pottery on "workboards," which were six feet long by nine inches across. The pots were brought from the warehouse to the decorating shop for painting. Quantities of ware were measured in the potteries in dozens. A piece-work rate was paid for a dozen items completed. Whereas a standard piece would be paid at twelve to the dozen, a complex and therefore time-consuming piece might only be four or five to the dozen, while a small and simple pot might rate eighteen to the dozen. This variable dozen counting method allowed a single rate of payment to cover both simple and complex making and decoration and is a system which dates back to the late 1600s and the earliest days of pottery manufacture in Staffordshire.

When the pattern had been outlined, the piece was passed on to a paintress who would fill in the colors. Each girl fetched her own paint in powder form from the paint shop, the number painted on the base of the pot she was about to decorate telling her which color in the manufacturer's series was required. She put a number of measures of color on a glazed tile with a measure of fat oil (concentrated turpentine). Water was then added, and the paint mixed with a palette knife to a thick consistency. The color was then painted on the pot, filling in the marked outlines. In some areas the color was solid and in some cases it was overlaid with etching strokes, using a wide flat brush cut crosswise and very dry paint. This gave a feathered effect. For many of the designs the piece was then passed to a "mottler," who filled in the background area with a small rubber sponge.

According to Emily Firmstone, a paintress from 1925:

> "It took about a quarter of an hour to put the pattern on, then about half an hour to paint it, then about ten minutes to mottle it, for an ordinary sized piece. You got about 1s 6d (7.5p) for painting it."

The ware then went into the kiln for the color to be hardened on, and on to the dipping house for glazing. Dipping was done by hand, the dipper having a tub of matt glaze in front of him, and also a tub on either side. One was of thicker, and the other of thinner, glaze. According to the hardness to which the piece had been biscuit fired before decoration, he would dip it into the appropriate tub. A pot that had been soft fired required a thinner glaze because it would be more porous and so absorb more of the glaze solution. A hard fired pot, being less absorbent, needed a thicker glaze to give the same result after the final firing. The matt glaze which was used had a high lead content. The dippers had to take daily iodine tablets and be examined regularly by a doctor because of the lead's poisonous effects. After dipping, the pots were placed in the glost oven, carefully ranged so that they did not touch, and each piece balanced on three stilts so that the base could be glazed, for final glost firing.

When the pots had been fired and removed from the kiln, there was a final inspection before they were stored in the warehouse until required for an order. Some vases were sent to silversmiths or metal mounters in Birmingham or Sheffield. There, silver or E.P.N.S. (Electro-Plated Nickel Silver) bands would be added to the rims to make an eye-catching contrast to the colored pottery.

The Pottery and Glass Record for August 1925 states of Clews that: "All Art Ware decorations are hand drawn and hand painted, and all are produced under the personal direction and supervision of the proprietors, Mr. P. S. Clews and Mr. H. B. Preece. They have another commendable attribute, no faulty or inferior pieces are allowed to leave the factory." Certainly it is true that employees were not permitted to purchase pottery, faulty or otherwise, at a reduced rate. However, a glance at some of the pieces found today will suggest that either standards were relaxed over the years, or that Mr. Clews

and Mr. Preece were not as vigilant as *The Pottery and Glass Record* imagined. Whereas most pots are beautifully and perfectly decorated, there are also those with mistakes in the pattern, areas missed, or painted in the wrong color. Underglaze chips at the base of a pot, or glaze faults where two pots have touched in the kiln are also sometimes found. A common problem is that a painted pattern which is sharply defined on one side of a pot is soft and ill-defined on the other side. According to Molly Brennan, a paintress in the 1920s, this was caused by the placing of the pot in the kiln during biscuit firing. If the ware received more heat on one side than the other, the hard fired side would not take the paint properly and it would then run during glost firing. She said "If ware was hard fired it would feel smooth and I would refuse to work on it because the colours run. Good ware felt rough and the paint would sink in." Alternatively, uneven or insufficient heat at the glost firing stage would also have caused the underglaze paint to run.

A jug which either received too much heat during biscuit firing, so that the color was not absorbed and ran on the surface of the clay, or did not receive enough heat at the glost firing stage, thus making the pattern "soft." The result is not unattractive, but neither is it what was intended. 8" x 5". $110-$130. £70-£80.

Most "faults" do not spoil the attractiveness of Chameleon Ware, and rather add to its hand-made charm. There are a few pieces, however, on which the pattern has run so much that only reference to the pattern number on the base (if legible) can reveal what was originally intended.

The Designs

Designs on Chameleon Ware are bold and bright. Some patterns are loosely based on flowers and leaves, but many are abstract and difficult to give a name to. No original pattern names have survived, but the base of each pot has a number which identifies both color and design. An example would be 61/113.

The first digits are the pattern number. Without a surviving pattern book, only patterns which have been found can be recorded, and the list is necessarily incomplete. Numbers seen range from 1-265, but have many gaps yet to be filled—or were maybe never allocated. I have recorded sixty-three individual numbered patterns but unfortunately not all patterns have numbers. The reason for this is not known, although stylistically the unnumbered patterns tend to be the later designs. In some cases they were probably trials which were not then put into production, but often quite frequently-found patterns are similarly not numbered.

The second three digits refer to the background color of the piece. The number is from the color manufacturer's trade list. Numbered colors are:

105 - green
113 - powder blue
116 - cobalt blue
117 - cream
125 - brown
127 - blue/gray, rarely seen

All numbered pattern pieces were painted with a background of one of the above colors. If the background has been so overlaid with colored pattern as to be unclear, the color of the base of the pot will be the numbered one. This system only applies to patterned ware. Plain pieces and art pottery glazed pieces do not have pattern numbers and many different colored glazes were used on these pots.

The pattern on this plate is no. 11 (flame) and its color is 125 (brown). The initials show that it was painted by L.R. (Laura Robinson).

45

Although Clews' pattern designs may be said to be original and different, a watch was obviously kept on other manufacturers' lines to see which were selling well; similar styles, although not direct copies, would then be brought out. Pattern no. 65 is Clews' attempt at the willow pattern—hardly classic, but attractive and interesting—in cobalt and white with a pagoda and willow tree. No. 23, which has a stylized house and willow trees with large catkins, is reminiscent of one of Clarice Cliff's designs. An unnumbered pattern, described in *The Pottery and Glass Record* of October 1933 as "A cream ground with floral patterns in blue, red and green" is so like the Poole pottery of the period as to be indistinguishable without reference to the base stamp. However, the majority of Clews designs were "all their own work," and the pieces are attractive in their own right and highly prized, both then and now.

Named Patterns

I have three pieces of Chameleon Ware in my collection which have names hand-painted on the base. They are Hereford, Salisbury, and Lichfield. Each of these is an English cathedral city, which might mean that this was the beginning of a series of named patterns. In each case I have an example of the same pattern on a different pot which is unnamed, so it would seem to have been a system which was not continued.

A superb set of coffee pot, sugar basin, milk jug, and six coffee cans and saucers in pattern 23, house and willow tree. The only set of this type and quality that I have ever seen. $800-$880. £500-£550.

Chapter 5
The Pottery Workers

There is no remaining record of the names of people who worked at Clews. I have listed those who were remembered by surviving paintresses as working at the pottery before the Second World War.

The Paintresses

Amongst many others (with mark, where known) were:

Laura Robinson   L.R.
Gertie Capper (Daniel Capper's daughter)
Hilda Jones
Minnie Jackson
Mary Matthews
Mary Brennan   M
Mary Littlehales
Hilda Pierce
Betty Brooks
Emily Firmstone   E or A (at different times)
May Whitehouse   12
Rebecca Moses
Lilly Nabond
Ada Alcock
Sadie Maskery
Cissie Hand   C
Miriam Bloor
Doris Matthews
Ada Wiggins
Nellie Hollins

Harriet Sproston
Joan Booth
Elsie Rock

Warehouse Women
Jennie Hancock
Hilda Cooper

Missus (Post-war)
Mrs. Windsor

Kiln Fireman
Mr. Owen

Joiner
Bill Stretton

Packer
George Thursfield

Teapot Makers
Bert Shelley
William Bloor

Works Manager (Post-war)
Arthur Machin

List of Paintress's Initials

and Numbers Seen

A	O	9
A2	R	12
B1	T	17
C	V	18
C1	W	20
E	X	32Y
L	Y.	37
L.R.	2	
M	4	
N	5	

When you first started, aged fourteen years, you used to keep 4d (1.7p) out of every 1/- (5p) you earned. Then when you were sixteen years, 8d (3.3p) out of the 1/- (5p), at eighteen years, 10d (4.2p) and then when you were twenty-one you were a journey woman, and what you had was yours, but you could never earn more than £1-10s-0d (£1.50) a week.

Letters usually appear in black and are the initials of the paintress who outlined the design. Where there is also a number, this is the mark of the paintress who filled in the color. The initials used were those of the first name of the paintress, but marks were only unique at any one time. Thus Emily might have the mark "E" but, if she left, then "E" could then become the mark of Edna. For this reason it has only been possible to put initials beside names with any confidence when they were given to me by the ladies themselves. If there were two paintresses with the same initial they could add a number after the letter, hence "C" and "C1".

Memories

Emily Firmstone, a paintress at Clews from 1925. Married Bert Shelley who made teapots for Clews.

I worked at Clews from 1925, and Mrs. Laura Robinson was over all the girls when I started to learn the trade. She left in 1932 and went to Sadlers. I went to the Burslem School of Art. Also Mr. Shelley, my husband, worked at Clews from the First World War as a teapot maker. He was there until it closed. The Chameleon Ware used to change colour when it was fired. To do it, you had a plain piece of ware, then you drew the pattern on, then you painted it, then it was mottled with a piece of rubber sponge in either blue, brown or green, then the kiln man would put it in the kiln to harden it on. Then it would go to the dipping house to be dipped, then in another kiln to have the final firing. I used to do all the best work. When I came out of my time, my mark was E or A.

Emily Firmstone (center) when a paintress at George Clews & Co. Ltd. in 1930.

I did some of the tracing. Mrs. Robinson had all the patterns in a book. She made them up by looking at books such as wallpaper ones, and fashion books or something on your pinafore, and took them from anything she thought would make a good pattern. Then she would show them to Mr. Preece and, if he liked them, she would do them. Mr. Preece was the other part of Clews. He was in the making and our (decorating) side. Mr. Clews was in the office end. They were hard times, but we enjoyed them. You could go out and leave your front door unlocked. You could go and get a basin from the warehouse and buy a 3d mixture of fish, chips and peas, then throw the basin on the shoreruck (tip) instead of washing it.

Sadie Smith née Maskery, a paintress at Clews 1925-1927.

I worked at Clews from 1925 to 1927, aged fourteen to sixteen, and started at 5/9d (28.7p) a week. I only worked for two years because we were laid off after the Christmas orders and the factory did not open again until more orders were taken at the March fair in Blackpool. I did the filling in and the sponging. I mostly worked on the flame pattern (no. 11). The paint was brushed on, but the etching strokes were done with a wide flat brush cut longwise. We put a little powder paint on a tile and worked it with a palette knife, which we had to buy ourselves, then added a drop of fat oil. I went on to work at Wilkinsons, and worked with Clarice Cliff.

May Nixon née Whitehouse, a paintress at Clews 1927-1930.

Arthur Machin was the Manager over the paintresses. He gave the orders to Laura Robinson, and she went to the warehouse with it. Hilda Cooper (warehouse manager) laid the orders out. They had been biscuit fired. Laura gave us a piece of paper with what we had to do written on it, and we went to fetch the pieces from the warehouse. Laura put the pattern on for us freehand. We mixed our own paints on a tile and painted the pots. I went to the Burslem Art School before I started at Clews.

Mary Richardson née Molly Brennan, a paintress at Clews.

Clews was a very happy little firm with about fifteen to twenty paintresses doing the decorated pots. Girls were taken on at fourteen, and paid about 6/- (30p) a week. Money was deducted from their wages for training. There was no mess room and nowhere to wash our hands, so we went round the ovens to keep warm and have a bit of fun at lunch time.

If the ware was hard fired I would refuse to work on it because the colours would run. When you were good at painting a pattern they kept you to it. Laura Robinson used to have all the new patterns to work on. When there are two painter's marks on the base of a pot, one is the tracer and one the filler-in. The pattern was done according to the first number and the colour according to the second.

Mr. Clews was a little man, no taller than me. He used to have a laugh and a joke with us. You would not think that he was the boss, he was not dressed up as you would expect an owner to be.

After you had finished your training, you were mostly on piece work and were paid by the dozen that you painted. The number in a dozen depended on how long each piece took to paint. I did a large piece for the Wembley Exhibition. For that I was on a day rate because it had to be done slowly and very carefully. It was a large pot in "Egyptian Fan" pattern (no. 22) in pale blue with a wide band at the top and base. I worked at Clews for quite a few years, but I had to give up painting in the end because my eyesight was getting bad.

Chapter 6
Chronology of George Clews & Co. Ltd.

Listing of types of pottery made by Clews and noted in *The Pottery Gazette* and *The Pottery and Glass Record:*

1914   Jet, samian, and Rockingham teapots. Art pottery—crystalline and opalescent glazes on white earthenware. Lustered, splashed, and veined vases. A semi-matt bronze rouge flambé. Hispano-Moresque patterns. A vellumed glaze with rouge flambé painting. An egg-shell glaze remindful of a robin's egg.

1915   Jet, samian, and Rockingham teapots, teapot sets, coffee pots, jugs etc. supplied in plain, decorated, mottled, and other styles. Art vases, flower pots, and bulb bowls in various metallic opaline, crystalline, and aventurine glazes. Also a raised line (slip-trailed) decoration, finished in rouge flambé.

1919   Jet, samian, and Rockingham teapots, mottled and in various painted styles. An all-green teapot. A chocolate colored pot with a broad cream slip band with a forget-me-not pattern. Shapes noted are Cresswell, Globe, Low Globe, Premier, and Antique. A Rockingham teapot with green leafage and a large white daisy. Samian ware with colored bands in blue, green, salmon, or white. Shaving mugs, in white with gold line or with litho spray and gold line.

1923   Displayed at Frank Findlay's Holborn showrooms: Vases and bowls in "a hedge sparrow's egg blue and a thrush's egg grey. The mottled green is very attractive too, as well as the mottled blue." A range of cube teapots in solid colors and also ordinary teapots.

1925   Displayed at the British Empire Exhibition, Wembley: Plaques, bowls and other ornamental lines—little morning sets, just two cups and saucers, sugar and cream. Decorative plates—six, eight, ten, and twelve inches across in Chameleon Ware.

"There is a soft greyish blue ground with conventional designs, also in subdued colours and a lustre finish. Ware supplied to metal and silversmiths in Sheffield, Birmingham and elsewhere for silver and electro-plate mounting.

A range of about 120 different shapes in vases, bowls, flower holders, and flower pots in Chameleon Ware. In utility ware, tobacco jars, jam jars, puff boxes, salad bowls, and candlesticks. Another special line is decoration in opalesque luster. A copy of an ancient Grecian lamp in various sizes and any color has "met with a ready sale."

1927   Hand-painted patterned ware (patterns no. 53, 61, and 22) illustrated in *The Pottery Gazette and Glass Trade Review.* Gold medal and diploma for "originality of design" at the Philadelphia Exhibition.

1929   Patent 327,254 accepted for non-drip teapot spout.

1930   Electric lamp bases—"a lemon ground tinged with sienna brown" and "orange crystalline, the shade being of orange silk to match." The lamps were made in a variety of sizes.

1931   Copies of Persian Art jugs and a Graeco-Celtic flagon. Rock garden reptiles introduced. "New glazes" on Chameleon Ware, notably blue streaked with orange.

1933   A new design in Chameleon Ware on a cream ground. A floral pattern in blue, red, and green. Also toast racks, condiment sets, and jam jars, as well as rock garden ornaments.

1934   Modern and dainty ashtrays, Nell Gwyn candlesticks, scent sprays, cigarette boxes. A new finish is a pretty mottled gray.

1936   Cube stoneware in "a pale matt oatmeal finish" made for the Cunard liner *Queen Mary*.

1939   "Compact" shape teapot and "Perfecto" sets, in mottled glaze. The IXL dripless teapot, sugar and cream sets, lager or lemonade sets. Various animals—Pekinese, Golden Setter, Scottie, and Bulldog. Hors d'oeuvre sets with round or square trays on an oak base.

1942   Death of Percy Clews.

1946   Cube stoneware supplied for the post-war re-fitting of the *Queen Elizabeth* ocean liner.

1947   The "Perfecto teapot set" advertised as "a streamlined teapot and hot water jug on an earthenware tray."

1950   "Tudor Rose." Designed for export only, Tudor Rose was a floral pattern on a white ground, with washband and gold lines. IXL - the non-drip teapot with metal spout produced for export and in small quantities for the home market.

21 July 1959   George Clews (Sales) Ltd. registered, as successors to George Clews & Co. Ltd.

1961   "Pirouette"—a new shape with a new range of colored glazes and under-glaze pattern effects. Also "Portobello," "Malacca," and "Safari" as new ranges.

July 1961   George Clews (Sales) Ltd. in liquidation. The end of the line for the company, after fifty-five years.

Chapter 7
Backstamps and Pattern Numbers

Backstamps

Without records from the firm it is not possible to give dates to backstamps. They are illustrated in the order in which I believe them to have been used, based on observation of the pots on which they have been noted.

A very early mark impressed into the base of the pot. The number 224 refers to the mold shape—in this case, a vase. This mark appears on the early art-glazed pieces.

The more usual early mark, also on a glaze effect pot. The "hand written" stamp was impressed into the base at the "green" stage, when the pottery had partially dried but before the biscuit firing. The glaze has collected in the impression, so that the words can be read. Three "stilt marks" can be clearly seen on this picture. These are left by the clay supports which prevented the base of the pot touching the saggar in the glost kiln.

The first design of printed mark which was put on the hand-painted patterned ware. The trade mark within the triangle is a chameleon.

An impressed "oddity" which appears on a hand-painted piece, just to show that all rules exist to be broken.

The second design, using a circle instead of a rectangle.

The "Clews circling the world" printed design, which was used on the non-Chameleon teapots and domestic ware.

The final printed stamp design for Chameleon Ware. This is probably the most common of the back stamps.

Pattern numbers

"Ginger Nutt." A children's transfer printed plate with a squirrel pushing a pram as its design. An example of Clews' diversification after the war, when hand painting was no longer done.

Many of the patterns were numbered, and those which I have identified are shown here. Without a pattern book or any type of sales catalog, the list contains only those patterns which I have seen during the past ten years. I have given each pattern a name. In a few cases they are in fairly general use among collectors (for example number 28, "squashed cat"), but mostly they are my own invention for ease of reference. It should be noted that these names were not used by Clews.

Not all patterns were produced in the same quantities. Obviously some were more popular and sold more successfully than others. I have rated each pattern to reflect its present day availability, from "very rare," through "rare," "uncommon," "fairly common," to "common." The following pictures show examples of individual patterns on particular pieces. It should be noted that the same pattern may look very different on another shaped piece, and also that the same pattern may be found in several different colors, only one of which is illustrated here.

Pattern 1 - mosaic. 4" x 3.5". $110-$145. £70-£90. Rare.

A later printed mark used on post-war pottery.

Pattern 6 - house in the woods. 7" x 5". $240-$320. £150-£200. Very rare.

Pattern 4 - blue/green sponging. 6.5" x 5.5". $40-$70. £25-£45. Fairly common.

Pattern 11 - flame. 7.5" x 6". $110-$145. £70-£90. Common; the best known Chameleon Ware pattern.

Pattern 12 - crocus petal. 12". $145-$175. £90-£110. Uncommon.

Pattern 13 - trefoil. 7" x 4". $110-$130. £70-£80. Uncommon.

Pattern 12 - pink/blue sponging. The pattern number 12 was used twice, probably in error. 3.5" x 9". $30-$50. £20-£30. Fairly common.

Pattern 18 - spade. 6" x 6.5". $145-$160. £90-£100. Rare.

Pattern 17 - pine cone with leaves. 9" x 5". $110-$145. £70-£90. Uncommon.

Pattern 19 - heart and scroll. 4.5" x 5". $105-$135. £65-£85. Uncommon.

Pattern 20 - palm tree. 9" x 5". $160-$190. £100-£120. Rare.

Pattern 22 - palm frond. 11" x 4.5". $120-$145. £75-£90. Common.

58

Pattern 25 - crown. 8" x 5.5". $160-$190. £100-£120. Uncommon.

Pattern 23 - house and willow tree. 8" x 5.5". $130-$150. £80-£95. Common.

Pattern 23 - curried egg. This pattern number was used twice, probably in error. 8.5". $160-$190. £100-£120. Rare.

Pattern 26 - Firebird. 6" x 3". $105-$120. £65-£75. Rare.

Pattern 27 - ghost dancers. 6" x 4". $70-$105. £45-£65. Uncommon.

Pattern 28 - dead cat (run over from the rear). 8" x 6". $160-$225. £100-£140. Common.

Pattern 27A - bean. 9" x 4". $135-$160. £85-£100. Uncommon.

Pattern 29 - autumn leaves. 4" x 9". $130-$160. £80-£100. Rare.

Pattern 32 - gazelle. 6" x 7". $120-$150. £75-£95. Uncommon.

Pattern 35 - thistle. 8" x 2.5". $80-$110. £50-£70. Uncommon.

Pattern 39 - chenille. 10". $145-$175. £90-£110. Uncommon.

Pattern 37 - junk. 5.5" x 4". $40-$55. £25-£35. Uncommon.

Pattern 40 - diamond. 8.5". $105-$120. £65-£75. Fairly common.

Pattern 44 - flower with spiky leaf. 8.5" x 8". $240-$320. £150-£200. Rare.

Pattern 48 - fir cone. 6.5" x 3.5". $120-$135. £75-£85. Uncommon.

Pattern 45 - shell. 13" x 6.5". $400-$480. £250-£300. Fairly common.

Pattern 50 - Mae West (look at the lips). 7" x 5". $160-$240. £100-£150. Common.

Pattern 50A - over-glaze painted Mae West pattern. Red, and this shade of green, were not available in colors which would stand the high temperature of the glost oven. They had to be painted over the glaze and fired on at a lower temperature in an enameling kiln. Pattern 50 was regularly painted in this variation. 9" x 4". $130-£160. £80-£100. Fairly common.

Pattern 59 - sea horses. 8.5" x 4". $120-$150. £75-£95. Rare.

Pattern 51 - flower with oil bubbles. 7" x 3.5". $120-$150. £75-£95. Rare.

Pattern 53 - owl. 6" x 4.5". $105-$120. £65-£75. Common.

Pattern 61 - holly leaf. 9" x 4". $145-$175. £90-£110. Common.

Pattern 62 - Christmas tree decorations. 9" x 4". $130-$160. £80-£100. Rare.

Pattern 63 - mustache. 6" x 4.5". $95-$110. £60-£70. Uncommon.

Pattern 65 - Chinese. 9" x 5.5". $225-$255. £140-£160. Fairly
common.

Pattern 80 - Greek key. 8.5" x 4.5". $145-$175. £90-£110. Fairly common.

Pattern 82 - rough sea. 3.5" x 8". $110-$145. £70-£90. Rare.

Pattern 83 - daisy. 6" x 7". $130-$160. £80-£100. Uncommon.

Pattern 84 - peacock tail. 7.5" x 3". $90-$120. £55-£75. Rare.

Pattern 91 - peony. 8.5" x 5". $175-$275. £110-£140. Common.

Pattern 85 - cat's whiskers. 3" x 4". $80-$95. £50-£60. Rare.

Pattern 92 - moon circles. 4.5" x 3.5". $80-$110. £50-£70. Uncommon.

Pattern 96 - flower and diagonal line. 8" x 5.5". $175-$225. £110-£140. Fairly common.

Pattern 95 - flower and oak leaf. 8" x 5.5". $160-$225. £100-£140. Uncommon.

Pattern 97 - blackberry with squared border. 10" x 9". $240-$320.
£150-£200. Uncommon.

Pattern 101 - Deco circle on green "leather bottle." 5.5" x 5".
$150-$190. £95-£120. Common.

Pattern 100 - flower circle on yellow "leather bottle." 5.5" x 5".
$150-$190. £95-£120. Uncommon.

Pattern 102 - Deco circle on brown "leather bottle." 5.5" x 5".
$150-$190. £95-£120. Common.

Pattern 201 - blackberry. 6" x 7". $130-$160. £80-£100. Common.

Pattern 105 - Deco circle on dark blue "leather bottle." 5.5" x 5".
$150-$190. £95-£120. Uncommon.

Pattern 202 - heart. 5.5" x 3". $80-$95. £50-£60. Uncommon.

Pattern 206 - modern flower. 9" x 5.5". $160-$210. £100-£130.
Fairly common.

Pattern 207 - African shield. 8" x 5.5". $145-$160. £90-£100. Fairly common.

Pattern 212 - tree blossom. 6" x 3.5". $110-$145. £70-£90. Uncommon.

Pattern 224 - hatched creeper. 9.5" x 4". $130-$160. £80-£100. Uncommon.

Pattern 227 - Persian flower on cream. 9" x 4.5". $120-$150. £75-£95. Uncommon.

Pattern 230 - tree lantern. 7.5" x 3". $80-$95. £50-£60. Uncommon.

Pattern 231 - star. 3.5" x 7". $120-$145. £75-£90. Uncommon.

Pattern 233 - blackberry leaf and diamond. 4" x 2.5". $50-$80. £30-£50. Uncommon.

Pattern 257 - Persian flower on blue. 9" x 4.5". $120-$150. £75-£95. Uncommon.

Chapter 8
Photo Essay

Large dark blue and brown vase. Pattern 61/116. 15" x 8". $400-$480. £250-£300.

Yellow/brown vase with the unusual variation of a fine dotted background. Pattern 50/125. 8" x 4". $145-$175. £90-£110.

A small round pot in green "flame" pattern. Clews' green is a complex color which is shaded and speckled with blue and brown. Pattern 11/105. 4.5" x 4.5". $105-$135. £65-£85.

A crisply painted pale blue jug. Pattern 61/113. 6.5" x 5". $130-$160. £80-£100.

Two differently shaped pots which do not take the pattern in exactly the same proportions. Pattern 22/113. Left: 10.5" x 4.5". $120-$150. £75-£95. Right: 7" x 3.5". $90-$120. £55-£75.

A tiny pot and a lipless jug which show the common but quite complex pattern of blue "flame." Pattern 11/113. Left: 2.5" x 3". $40-$55. £25-£35. Right: 8" x 5.5". $145-$175. £90-£110.

A large vase in rich brown tones. As might be expected with such a beautifully decorated piece, its base is marked with "L.R." by Laura Robinson. Pattern 91/125. 14.25" x 7". $480-$560. £300-£350.

A simple pale blue bowl with an unusual edging of flowers, seed pods, and leaves, in dark blue. No pattern number. 2.5" x 10". $70-$90. £45-£55.

A pleasantly shaped blue and brown vase. Pattern 53/116. 10.5" x 6". $225-$290. £140-£180.

A candle stick with a practical wide base. Although the decoration is brown and blue, the white interior shows that the color number 117 (i.e., cream) is correct. Pattern 40/117. 4.5" x 4.5". $120-$150. £75-£95.

A tall and elegant "double" vase, beautifully painted by Laura Robinson. Pattern 91/113. 14.5" x 6". $400-$480. £250-£300.

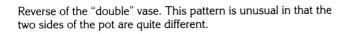

Reverse of the "double" vase. This pattern is unusual in that the two sides of the pot are quite different.

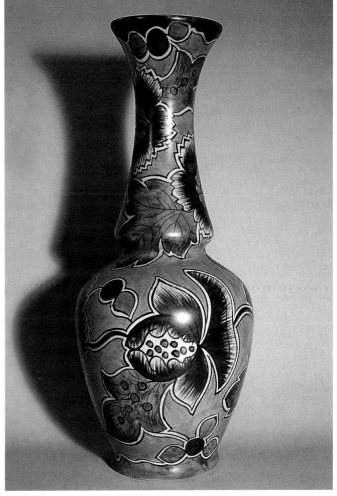

A pale blue vase, pattern 39/113. 7" x 3". $120-$145. £75-£90.

This "Mae West" pattern looks particularly attractive in brown, using a very 1930s range of tones. Pattern 50/125. 9" x 4". $130-$150. £80-£95.

Three pieces show the same "Mae West" pattern arranged on different shapes. Pattern 50/125. Large vase: 9" x 5.5". $145-$175. £90-£110. Small vase: 6" x 4". $80-$95. £50-£60. Bowl: 2.5" x 10". $105-$120. £65-£75.

No pattern number. On-glaze painting on marbled background. This little pot has been heavily loaded with a marble glaze, then a bobbled fringe design added after the first firing. 4.5" x 2.5". $40-$55. £25-£35.

A pair of vases and a wall plate in the same pale blue "trefoil" pattern look quite different as the design is expanded or contracted to fit round the shape. Pattern 13/113. Plate: 12". $190-$255. £120-£160. Vases: 7" x 4". $225-$255. £140-£160 for pair.

A large and imposing pot which has been decorated
in rich shades of brown. Pattern 19/125. 14.5" x 9".
$480-$560. £300-£350.

A set of six pots in the "Chinese" pattern. Each has been turned to show a different part of the design which
goes all round the pot. Pattern 65/117. Largest: 14.5" x 7.5". $480-$640. £300-£400. Smallest: 4" x 3.5". $130-
$150. £80-£95.

The painting on this vase is rather coarse, without the delicate brush strokes seen on some Chameleon Ware. Pattern 48/117. 7" x 4". $110-$145. £70-£90.

A brown vase on which the brush strokes used to fill in the plain area are very obvious. This was intentional, to show that the ware was decorated by hand. Pattern 22/125. 10.5" x 5". $145-$175. £90-£110.

A selection of dark blue "flame" pattern pieces. The design has been adapted to fit concave, convex, and flat shapes. Pattern 11/116. Plate: 12". $240-$320. £150-£200.

A large and a small bowl, shown with a lidded soup bowl. Plain mottled green glaze. Large bowl: 3" x 7.5". $65-$80. £40-£50. Small bowl: 2" x 3.5". $25-$30. £15-£20. Soup bowl: 3" x 7". $30-$40. £20-£25.

A simply painted pale blue vase with an abstract pattern. No pattern number. 6" x 3". $80-$95. £50-£60.

A wall plate and a small pot, in a cream glaze with pastel decoration. No pattern number, but a variation of pattern 50. Plate: 12". $130-$160. £80-£100. Pot: 4" x 3.5". $65-$80. £40-£50.

A variation of pattern 50/129. The color number 129 is rarely found, but refers to a pale gray/blue. 7" x 4". $110-$145. £70-£90.

A straight sided vase, well painted in an unusual design. Pattern 63/117. 7" x 4". $145-$175. £90-£110.

A complex pattern for a small vase. This pattern is more usually seen in brighter colors. Pattern 96/117. 6.5" x 3". $110-$145. £70-£90.

No pattern number. Raised slip trailed (tube lined) pattern. 9" x 5". $145-$160. £90-£100.

The dark blue "flame" pattern is shown to advantage on this large vase which is flanked by a smaller pair. Pattern 11/116. Large vase: 15.25" x 8". $480-$545. £300-£340. Small vases: 7" x 4". $290-$320. £180-£200 for pair.

This design includes areas of bright yellow, a color not regularly found on Chameleon Ware. Pattern 96/117. Plate: 12". $240-$320. £150-£200.

The "diamond" pattern on three quite different shapes. Pattern 40/117. Plate: 8.5". $105-$120. £65-£75.

Three examples of the "holly" pattern, including a large double vase. Each has the paintress mark "L.R." on its base. Pattern 61/125. Tall vase: 14.5" x 5". $480-$560. £300-£350. Vase: 9" x 4". $145-$175. £90-£110. Plate: 8". $145-$175. £90-£110.

The "tree blossom" pattern has a zigzag border. Although not seen in this picture, it circles the top outer edge of the bowl. Pattern 212/117. Vase: 6" x 3.5". $110-$145. £70-£90. Bowl: 3" x 9". $90-$120. £55-£75.

A finely painted straight sided vase. Vertical surfaces show a design without distortion. Pattern 35/113. 9" x 4.5". $160-$225. £100-£140.

A beautifully decorated large "Chinese" vase. Although Clews' version of the willow pattern is by no means classic, it has a freedom of interpretation, yet includes the basic elements of the design. Pattern 65/117. 14.5" x 8". $560-$640. £350-£400.

92

Various patterns on shape no. 207. This unusual shape is most attractive and forms a small collection on its own. 6" x 5". $105-$135. £65-£85 each.

A sugar sifter with on-glaze painting of an Alpine scene. An oddity, unlike anything else in the Clews range. 5" x 3". $55-$70. £35-£45.

Detail from the "Alpine" sugar sifter.

An unusual freely painted pot. Probably a late piece, judging by the style of decoration. No pattern number. 7" x 5". $120-$150. £75-£95.

This vase shows the house in the "house and willow tree" design. Pattern 23/117. 7" x 4". $80-$110. £50-£70.

Black, and shades of brown, have been used to form the pattern on this vase. Brown Chameleon Ware often has areas of green in the design but, on this pot, green has not been used. Pattern 44/125. 8" x 3". $145-$175. £90-£110.

A simple cream stipple-effect pot with blue edging. Pattern 12/117. 3.5" x 6". $40-$55. £25-£35.

Two attractive and practical lamp bases. The small tray on which each appears to be standing is joined to the lamp base. Left: Pattern 53/116. Right: Pattern 11/125. 8" x 7.5". $175-$240. £110-£150 each.

A small green ash or pin tray, in which excess glaze has unfortunately pooled, hiding some of the design. Pattern 202/105. 1" x 4". $40-$55. £25-£35.

A pale blue plate. Probably too small to be intended for wall decoration, but not produced in sets for daily use either. Pattern 17/113. 8". $90-$120. £55-£75.

The "flame" pattern was applied to pieces of all shapes and sizes, and always looks right wherever it is found. Pattern 11/116. Left: 7" x 3". $80-$110. £50-£70. Right: 5.5" x 4". $80-$110. £50-£70.

Three plain glazed bowls. Blue: Color 116. Brown: Color 125. Green: Color 105. Approximately 3" x 8". $65-$95. £40-£60 each.

The "house and willow tree" pattern is in the style of some of Clarice Cliff's designs. Pattern 23/117. Plate: 12". $190-$225. £120-£140. Large pot: 8" x 9". $240-$270. £150-£170.

The "flame" design on this large pot has been fairly crudely applied. The flame is short and rounded instead of long and elegant, and the shaded etching strokes are hardly there. Whoever painted this, it was certainly not "L.R." Pattern 11/113. 8" x 9". $270-$305. £170-£190.

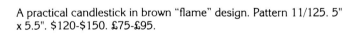

A practical candlestick in brown "flame" design. Pattern 11/125. 5" x 5.5". $120-$150. £75-£95.

A most beautiful lidded ginger jar, painted in "peony" pattern in brown by "L.R." Every area of the design is perfectly executed. Pattern 91/125. 10" x 9". $720-$800. £400-£450.

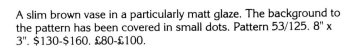

A slim brown vase in a particularly matt glaze. The background to the pattern has been covered in small dots. Pattern 53/125. 8" x 3". $130-$160. £80-£100.

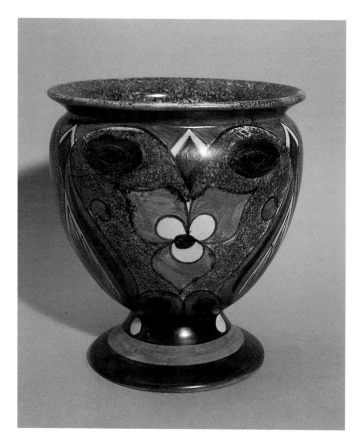

An urn, or perhaps a rose bowl, as the inside is plain pale blue. An interesting shape, which shows the design to advantage. Pattern 53/116. 7" x 6". $160-$210. £100-£130.

A large, well painted vase, which has a fairly small area of actual pattern but a large area covered by the two bands which are associated with this design. Pattern 28/125. 12" x 8". $240-$320. £150-£200.

A "Chinese" pot. This side features the temple, the willow tree, and the bridge, which are usually associated with the willow pattern. Underglaze painting does not allow for detail in representation, but the idea is made clear. Pattern 65/117. 9" x 8". $320-$400. £200-£250.

A pot which typifies Chameleon Ware at its best. Crisply painted in browns and yellows, and well glazed. Pattern 53/125. 10" x 7". $160-$190. £100-£120.

At first glance, a pair, but in fact two similar designs on the same shape vase. Left: Pattern 61/116. Right: Pattern 27A/116. 8" x 6.5". $145-$175. £90-£110 each.

On this wall plate, the entire "peony" design fits on one surface instead of half being hidden on the rear of a pot. A superb design, beautifully painted. Pattern 91/116. 12". $320-$400. £200-£250.

A lidded powder bowl in plain pale blue—"plain" meaning that there is no painted pattern. The speckled glaze is interesting and attractive, and anything but plain. Color 113. 5.5" x 5.5". $50-$65. £30-£40.

Two large and good looking vases in the "Greek key" design. Pattern 80/113. Left: 8" x 4.5". $175-$210. £110-£130. Right: 10.5" x 6.5". $225-$270. £140-£170.

When flattened out to decorate a plate, this design looks very different from when it appears on a vase. Pattern 53/125. 8.5". $95-$110. £60-£70.

No pattern number. A "Poole Pottery" look-alike. The colors used on these designs are quite different from the standard Chameleon Ware range. The hand painting is much more freely done, and does not involve filling in an outlined shape. 8.5" x 6". $160-$190. £100-£120.

Named on the base "Lichfield," an English cathedral city, this vase has a broken line decoration around the top, as usually found on Poole pottery of the 1930s. Only the base mark confirms that it is Chameleon Ware. 6.5" x 6.5". $160-$190. £100-£120.

A delicate "Poole" design. The small pot has "Hereford," an English cathedral city, marked on the base. Left: 11" x 8.5". $320-$385. £200-£240. Right: 5.5" x 4.5". $80-$95. £50-£60.

An unusual shape which is almost a globe. The design fits on it well. Pattern 27/116. 4" x 5". $130-$160. £80-£100.

Pattern 61/125. Both these pots have the same pattern and color numbers, but they look quite different. Left: 10" x 7.5". $190-$225. £120-£140. Right, the spotted version: 8" x 6". $145-$175. £90-£110.

Flat bowls like this one were very popular in the 1930s. They were filled with water and flowers were floated on the surface. This pale blue bowl has a central design which looks good either when viewed through water or when the bowl is empty. Pattern 39/113. 3" x 10". $130-$160. £80-£100.

Pattern 65/117. A "Chinese" willow pattern powder bowl, with the knob in the form of an oriental man. 4.5" x 4.5". $160-$190. £100-£120.

A small rectangular trinket box, decorated with the dark blue "flame" pattern. It is unusual to see this design applied to a piece with square corners and straight edges. Pattern 11/116. 2" x 5". $120-$150. £75-£95.

No pattern number. A stylized leaping gazelle or ibex, on an unusual brown background with colored flowers. All on-glaze painted and a little odd and unlike other Chameleon Ware designs. Left: 10" x 8". $145-$175. £90-£110. Right: 6" x 7". $120-$150. £75-£95.

The rich brown color gives these examples of the "crocus petal" design a strong 1930s appearance. Pattern 12/125. Large plate: 12". $160-$240. £100-£150. Small plate: 7". $90-$105. £55-£65.

A selection of large and small examples of pattern 53/116 in blue. Center vase: 10.5" x 6". $225-$290. £140-£180.

Two short oil lamps. They have the same lids as tall oil lamps, and share with them the problem of broken knobs. Left: Pattern 50/125. Right: Pattern 11/125. 3.5" x 6.5". $145-$175. £90-£110 each.

Various small pieces of Chameleon Ware. Tallest: 7" x 4".

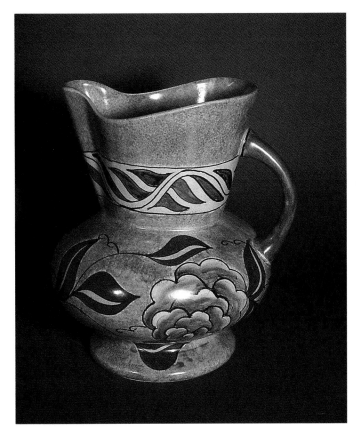

A large brown water jug which would hold water for the table, or look good displaying a large bunch of daffodils in the spring. Pattern 50/125. 10" x 7.5". $145-$175. £90-£110.

Detail of a vase, showing the original adhesive metallic paper label.

A dark blue vase with the "Egyptian fan" pattern. The yellow used on this pattern gives a particularly good contrast and the simple rounded shape takes the design well. Pattern 22/116. 7" x 5". $145-$175. £90-£110.

On Chameleon Ware, the design is always expanded to fill the available space. The "Mae West" pattern in browns and muted green looks just right on this jug. Pattern 50/125. 8" x 5.5". $145-$175. £90-£110.

A most unusual color variation of the "fir cone" design. A dark blue background filled in with fine brown dots adds to the interest. Pattern 48/116. 7" x 5". $120-$150. £75-£95.

A dark brown "flame" patterned plate which shows the design in all its intricacy. Pattern 11/125. 12". $175-$240. £110-£150.

A tall oil lamp in dark blue. Pattern 28/116. 8" x 6.5". $240-$320. £150-£200 (value is for a lamp with lid intact. Very many are broken at the knob, or are missing the lid completely).

A tall oil lamp in patterned brown. This shape must have been popular, as it is found in many different patterns as well as most of the plain colors. Pattern 53/125. 8" x 6.5". $240-$320. £150-£200 (with lid intact).

Another tall oil lamp in patterned brown. Because of their tall and elegant shape, these pieces are often found with damage, and not many have survived intact. Pattern 50/125. 8" x 6.5". $240-$320. £150-£200 (with lid intact).

An unusual ribbed vase in green "flame" design. Pattern 11/105. 9" x 7.5". $160-$190. £100-£120.

A brown bowl with loosely painted turquoise circles round the outer surface. No pattern number. 3.5" x 8". $50-$65. £30-£40.

An un-numbered leaf design. The large vase has "Salisbury," an English cathedral city, on the base. 7.5" x 5". $105-$135. £65-£85. Small vase: 5" x 4". $40-$50. £25-£30.

Pattern 22/125, showing the varying way that the same pattern has been adapted to fit different shapes. Bowl: 2" x 10.5". $145-$190. £90-£120. Plate: 8.5". $110-$130. £70-£80. Vase: 10.5" x 5". $145-$175. £90-£110.

With most Chameleon Ware patterns, the standard of painting is quite variable, but the "peony" design is always beautifully reproduced. Perhaps its complexity meant that it was only attempted by experienced paintresses. This large pot is quite perfect. Pattern 91/113. 13" x 8". $480-$560. £300-£350.

A short candlestick which would be most practical in use. Pattern 61/116. 2" x 4". $70-$90. £45-£55.

Pattern 50A/113. On this variation of pattern 50, the red and green areas are colored with on-glaze painting, done after the first firing. This gives an added color range to a pattern which comes in many different color variations. Vase: 9" x 4". $145-$175. £90-£110. Box: 3" x 5". $105-$135. £65-£85.

No pattern number. A fairly late piece by the style, which has been painted on a slightly ribbed vase. 8" x 5.5". $130-$160. £80-£100.

Various small pieces of blue Chameleon Ware.

The stylized tree design on a fawn background. 7" x 4". $95-$110.
£60-£70.

A design of stylized trees on a small pale blue pot and a pale green
bowl. No pattern number. Left: 4.5" x 5". $70-$90. £45-£55. Right:
4" x 8". $65-$80. £40-£50.

No pattern number. This large vase is a variation of pattern 50, in pale pastel colors. 14.5" x 7". $270-$335. £170-£210.

The dark blue "crown" design has here been flattened out to decorate a wall plate. Pattern 25/116. 10". $175-$210. £110-£130.

A tall and impressive vase in the "owl" design. This angle shows the two eyes and diamond shaped beak which give the pattern its name. Pattern 53/116. 14.5" x 10". $480-$560. £300-£350.

No pattern number. An unusually restrained design for Chameleon Ware. Autumn leaves are painted on-glaze, under the lip of the vase. 7" x 4". $90-$105. £55-£65.

Two vases decorated in a dark blue glaze, mottled with brown. Left: 8" x 3.25". $70-$90. £45-£55. Right: 7.5" x 3". $65-$70. £40-£45.

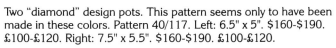

Two "diamond" design pots. This pattern seems only to have been made in these colors. Pattern 40/117. Left: 6.5" x 5". $160-$190. £100-£120. Right: 7.5" x 5.5". $160-$190. £100-£120.

A "Chinese" pattern vase, showing the rear of the design with a rising sun and two banners. Pattern 65/117. 8.5" x 8". $400-$480. £250-£300.

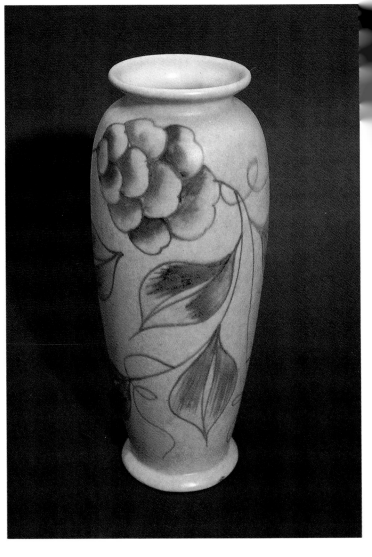

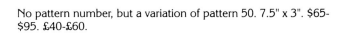

No pattern number, but a variation of pattern 50. 7.5" x 3". $65-$95. £40-£60.

This unusual circle and straight line design completely covers a rounded jug. Pattern 92/117. 6" x 4.5". $120-$150. £75-£95.

The "etching strokes" done with a wide dry brush shade brown into green in the centre of this design. Pattern 95/105. 7" x 4". $175-$190. £110-£120.

A selection of pieces in pale blue "flame" design. Probably the best known of all the Chameleon Ware patterns. Pattern 11/113.

A "Chinese" pattern vase, showing the flower at the front of the design. Pattern 65/117. 6" x 3.5". $130-$175. £80-£110.

A glossy glazed lilac bowl. 4" x 9.5". $55-$70. £35-£45.

A lamp base with a cream-colored background, over-painted with a part sunburst pattern. Although Clews acknowledged the Art Deco style in many of their designs, few were as aggressively Deco, either in shape or in decoration, as this one. 13" x 6". $30-$50. £20-£30.

A plate with a delicate (for Clews) rose in the center. 7". $30-$40. £20-£25.

Pattern 80/113. The pattern has run under the glaze on this pot, bending the straight lines of the border. 10" x 10". $160-$240. £100-£150.

The "blackberry" design is one of the few which appear on green Chameleon Ware. The reason for this is unknown. Pattern 201/105. Left: 5" x 4". $70-$90. £45-£55. Center: 5.5" x 5". $90-$105. £55-£65. Right: 2.5" x 7". $145-$160. £90-£100.

A large and beautiful lamp base decorated in the brown "owl" design. Pattern 53/125. 9" x 8". $400-$480. £250-£300.

A rare shape for Chameleon Ware. This bulb bowl shows the pale blue "flame" design stretched out along the side. Pattern 11/113. 2.5" x 12". $210-$255. £130-£160.

A round trinket box in dark blue. Although the lid fits the base perfectly, they have different pattern numbers. The base appears to be decorated with the band design from pattern 50, whilst the lid has a reduced version of pattern 22, "palm frond". Pattern of base: 14/116. Pattern of lid: 22/116. 2.5" x 4". $95-$130. £60-£80.

A small vase decorated with a simple flower and leaf design has been given a brown luster glaze over the pattern. No pattern number. 4.5" x 2.5". $90-$105. £55-£65.

The single peony flower takes up the whole of one side of this small vase. Pattern 91/113. 4" x 5". $145-$160. £90-£110.

A brown fruit bowl decorated on the outside with the "Mae West" design. Pattern 50/125. 3.5" x 8.5". $90-$120. £55-£75.

A small lidded bowl, perhaps intended for a dressing table, in dark blue "flame" design. The knob on the lid is an oriental man. Pattern 11/116. 4" x 4.5". $145-$160. £90-£100.

A handled bowl in brown "owl" design. Pattern 53/125. 4" x 11". $130-$160. £80-£100.

A "plain" blue vase in Clews' beautiful cobalt semi-matt glaze. The unusual shape of this pot shows the streaky crystalline glaze to perfection. 4" x 5". $65-$80. £40-£50.

An oatmeal glazed pot with an unusual swirled design which gives a three-dimensional effect. Alternatively it could represent bunches of bananas ripening in a room with cobwebs. The interpretation is left to the viewer! 9" x 6.5". $120-$150. £75-£95.

An unusual color range with a brown dotted background gives a different look to a fairly common design. Pattern 53. 6" x 4". $110-$130. £70-£80

This plate is not, at first sight, obviously by Clews, but something made me take a closer look as I walked past it at an antique fair. The only mark on the back of the plate is "105". A hopeful sign, because 105 on a Clews piece implies a green background. On the front of the plate the green is mottled with blue and yellow, another good sign, as Clews' green is rarely a single color. Conversely, it has a heavily embossed design and border pattern which I had not seen before, but it felt "right" and I was sufficiently convinced to buy the plate—particularly as, without a maker's mark, it was inexpensive. Not until I got it home did I realize that, apart from some extra fern leaves, the pattern is number 97 (blackberry leaf and squared border). An unusual plate, embossed in the mold with the pattern hand-decorated. It was probably intended to hang on the wall. 10". $30. £20 was the price I paid for the plate. If I were to sell it, however, I would ask several times that price.

A really magnificent plant holder which shows the dark blue "flame" design perfectly. Pattern 11/116. 10" x 13". $320-$400. £200-£250.

Bibliography

Baker, Diane. *Potworks: The Industrial Architecture of the Staffordshire Potteries*. London: Royal Commission on the Historical Monuments of England, 1991.

Buckley, Cheryl. *Potters and Paintresses: Women Designers in the Pottery Industry 1870-1955*. London: The Women's Press, 1990.

Megaw, J.V.S., and M. Ruth Megaw. *The Basse-Yutz Find: Masterpieces of Celtic Art*. Reports of the Research Committee of the Society of Antiquaries of London. No. XLVI. London: The Society of Antiquaries of London. Distributed by Thames and Hudson Ltd., 1990.

Sarsby, Jacqueline. *Missuses & Mouldrunners: An Oral History of Women Pottery-Workers at Work and at Home*. London and Philadelphia: Open University Press, 1988.

The Pottery and Glass Record
First published 1918;
not published April 1940-October 1944;
became *Pottery and Glass*, November 1944;
became *Tableware*, January 1963;
incorporated into *The Pottery Gazette and Glass Trade Review*, July 1964.

The Pottery Gazette
First published 1877;
became *The Pottery Gazette and Glass Trade Review*, January 1919;
incorporated into *Tableware*, July 1964;
became *Tableware International*, 1970.

Tableware International. Published by DMG Business Media Ltd. Redhill, Surrey, Great Britain.

Index